Seasons of the Witch

Primer

a companion guide

by Victoria David Danann

Seasons of the Witch PRIMER
by Victoria David Danann

second edition, copyright © 2007.
Published by 7th House Publishing, The Woodlands, Texas.

7th House Publishing
395 Sawdust Road, #2029
The Woodlands, TX 77380
www.7th-House.com
mail@7th-House.com

First Edition
First Printing
1-933320-11-7
Printed in the U.S.

My dog and I made our way along the forest path this morning just past sunrise. As we turned the bend just before Snake Creek we came upon a fully grown Great Blue Heron. Though four-feet-tall he was on a slight rise so that he and I surveyed each other at eye level. For almost a minute he stood as still as a statue before spreading six-foot wings and rising silently into the air. I wondered what he was thinking about us. He did not speak, but I heard him say, "It's going to be a magickal day."

Indeed.

Seasons of the Witch PRIMER: A Companion Guide

Foreword

The Orientation of Seasons of the Witch

In mid 1999 I completed development on a witch's planner unlike anything done before. I had developed a method, now termed my PowerCast™ system, for identifying optimal days and times for particular aspects of my practice such as spellcasting, meditation, working in my Book of Shadows and so forth. This I melded with the modern notion of organizers to create an ultimate planner for cross-tradition, practice of the craft.

The first ever witch's day planner was released by 7th House in September of 2001. In 2003 we added the Weekly version. In 2004 we published an abbreviated version of *Seasons* in wall calendar format for the first time. Our reviews, by both media and customers, have been lavish with praise. 7th House Publishing now operates as a small, family owned and run establishment which I lovingly call a "witch's cottage industry".

Seasons of the Witch is about the practice of magick and not about the practice of a particular pagan path. It is designed for use by cross-tradition pagans. It leans toward Wicca, partly for economic reasons, because the majority of our users identify themselves as Wiccan. Still, even Wicca is a "big tent" designation with lots of room for diversity. I try to include something useful for pagans in general.

Although we create an electronic version of *Seasons of the Witch*, I hope there will always be people like myself who get satisfaction from the touch of paper and the creative participation of writing.

Seasons of the Witch has been an immeasurable blessing for me. In this case, the law of three closer resembles three hundred and three. I receive letters from people with stories that are nothing less than astounding to me. I will never know whether these effects are a subconscious projection of the owner's power and wishes onto the books or whether the books actually accrue their own essential, magickal qualities because of my desire to add substance to the lives of *Seasons'* users. The answer could be both, or a combination of the two, or there may be a third, unknown factor at work.

One woman wrote to tell me she held her *Seasons of the Witch* close to her heart while her husband underwent surgery. She said her intuition told her that the close proximity of the book would give her comfort and strength necessary to cope with the events to pass.

A co-owner of Heart of the Dragon in Grand Junction, Colorado told me that they look forward to the arrival of the new *Seasons of the Witch* inventory each year because they sense that it raises the energy level in the store.

An office worker told me she was having problems with an office clique that was circulating damaging gossip about her. She responded with feelings of anxiety, insecurity and general disquiet. She said she received her copy of *Seasons* and took it to work with her thinking that she would lay the groundwork for a casting. She set the planner next to her computer and says that problems evaporated immediately without the need for further action. Even though my first inclination is to suspect that this would have occurred regardless, as these things often have short-lived cycles, I relate the story as told to me.

In the interest of sparing you a complete recounting, I will skip to the last, but not least. Of all the comments that have come my way, my favorite was made by a soror who wrote to say she loves *Seasons* so much that she plans to take it with her to Summerland and, failing that, she will reincarnate and buy it in her future lives.

Introduction

Looking for the truth.

Some would say traditional witchcraft has been "tainted" by exposure to the mysticism of the East. My view is that presently there is only one spiritual group that holds itself available for recognition, reception, absorption and, if necessary, revision in the interest of a whole truth. This group, though diverse, has migrated toward a spiritual outpost called pagan. All others have committed to systems which, though flawed by their own admission, are stagnant by definition of not growing. Further, on the issue of stagnation, it is utterly impossible, given the laws of physics, to stand still or stay in the same place. You are either moving forward or you're moving backward. This applies to everything including matters of spirit.

I am starting from the premise that the truth of our origins, our capabilities and our destinies is a puzzle with pieces scattered all over the earth, some found in the remains or race memories of collective experience, some found by encounters with nonhuman benefactors, some found by the practice of trial and error, and, perhaps, just to keep it intriguing, some not to be found at all. A closed system doesn't just resist the search for missing pieces. A closed system forbids it.

A closed system feeds on ignorance and abdication of spiritual responsibility due to fear and laziness. As an example of both, I wouldn't be surprised to find that not one Christian in ten thousand has actually read the entire Bible cover to cover. Christians are not encouraged to read the Bible cover to cover because, if they did, there would be a lot more hard, hard, hard questions. Tradition is a poor substitute for a search for truth. When a person elevates tradition above a desire to find the truth, they have abdicated responsibility for their own spiritual well-being. Like "faith", tradition is an enemy of truth. There is salvation, but it is not a salvation from the hell fires and brimstone of folk stories. It is salvation from a meaningless life and it can be found in quest, the noblest pursuit to which humans may aspire.

American pagans have adopted perspectives, terminology and practices that would seem foreign and strange to the European practitioners of the past and many of the present as well. Who are these occupants of an outpost who would seek to light a beacon torch to light the way toward the discovery of truth? Not "truth" as manipulative buzz word used by those who should be proscribed (charismatic charlatans and rigid theologians who exploit the word "truth" for the purpose of power, ego or treasure), but truth in the pure sense of incontrovertible principle. It would seem logical that Americans, as the cultural product of multiculturalism, would be intellectually predisposed to flexibility. This is true of those Americans who have had the opportunity to benefit from some of the positive aspects of multiculturalism. In other words, it would not be true where communities are largely one race or ethnicity and/or one religion.

Magick is the richest, most fertile ground for truth-seeking that I know. Real magick challenges the individual to take responsibility for what they choose to believe and how they will apply those beliefs. Real magick is not a process of following a prescribed checklist like a cooking recipe. Real magick requires a unique contribution as can only be made by the individual who is practicing. The nature of real magick dictates that no two spells (that work) would or should or could ever be the same.

A true witch turns stones over without fear of seeing what may hide underneath. A true witch is not a "sheep in the fold". A true witch is not an ant in a colony. A true witch will always be her/his ultimate authority. While you may be part of a group or system of study, while you may submit to the wisdom of the more experienced, while you may supplicate in the interest of perfecting your craft, the ultimate decision about what you believe and what you practice must remain your prerogative alone. A true witch has an inner voice which cannot be betrayed without consequence. One possible consequence, perhaps the most tragic, is the loss of that inner compass; that voice that is silenced and not heard again. In final analysis, you must serve as your own priest.

I encourage you to take away from this writing what may be of use to you. This work is an expression of education and experience. It is not a gospel, but it may have some pieces of truth.

While it was not my intention to write a book about me, I found it useful to include a few personal vignettes. Our conclusions are, after all, a result of our experiences.

The Book's Blessing

Before January begins you will find in your planner a page called *The Book's Blessing*. It is a love letter written to the owner of the book using the best template and most powerful magick I know; to want for each of you what I want for myself. This is the one and only place where you will ever find that I used the term "witch's diary". It is a poetic reference in honor of the language of those who have gone before.

The books have been blessed collectively. That may not keep you safe from every harm or disappointment, but, perhaps it shouldn't as these things are powerful building blocks to wisdom.

CONTENTS

Seasons of the Witch PRIMER: A Companion Guide

SECTION I

My Theory of Magick

*The only thing I can know for
certain is that we're all experiencing
a different reality and
that truth is a moving target.*

If you want to practice magick,
you must learn to be still.

If you live behind a wall of sound,
and cannot be alone with your own thoughts
you are not worthy to call on The Source.

Chapter 1   The Hard Questions

Notes on the origins of spells. Before I begin with answers to some of the hard questions, I must make a statement regarding the origins of the actual spells you will use. Although I do believe that it is possible for one person to perform a spell for another in exchange for value, monetary or otherwise, I do not think the result is likely to be remarkable. Likewise, I do not think that prepackaged spells are the best approach. The saying you pay for what you get is never more true.

Magick can only deliver the big bang, which is personal growth and accomplishment, if you pay the required price which means doing the work yourself. In other words, write your own spell, choose and gather your own materials, be your own priest. You can use someone else's idea for inspiration, but your spell will be hollow if not infused by your own desire, intention and emotion.

It's simple. You put a little in, you get a little out.
You put a lot in, you get a lot out.

1. *What is Magick?*

Magick and Science.

It has been postulated that science and magick are on a trajectory course to intersect at some point in the future. One bit of magickal lore relates that the Creatrix made a thirteenth sign of the zodiac which would be named and revealed at the time when astrology and astronomy enter an alliance of cooperation and mutual respect. There will certainly be a time when that which we may now call magick, or supernatural, or extra-normal, will be explained in Science classes with the casual ease of relating Newtonian physics. Doubts surrounding the authenticity of magickal events will be as laughable as stories of jungle natives making "gods" of travelers bearing cigarette lighters. Until then, you can expect the scientific community to be, not just skeptical, but contemptuous of what cannot be proven using "scientific method".

Since my theory of magick cannot, at present, be "proved" by replicable test, it will most likely remain a theory until long after my demise. On what can we agree now? We believe, meaning both scientists and witches, that everything in the multi-verse is composed of energy and that physical form is an expression of "trapped" energy. Both communities agree that the relationships and movements of objects in the heavens effect the emotions of Earth's inhabitants and, consequently, events both large and small. The most common example of this is the waxing and waning of our moon.

The scientific community will not easily reverse what they have ridiculed for centuries because of the legitimate fear of appearing to be very silly indeed. Even that which can be proven using their own criteria; a version of "beating them at their own game", is only reluctantly elevated to the status of "fact". For instance, if it may be proved statistically that there are more car accidents, emergency room visits, homicides, etc. each month during the hours of the full moon, the scientific community may agree that this is a verifiable, statistical phenomenon. While you may think that a reasonable person, upon reviewing this information, would conclude that there is a direct relationship between humankind and the movements of heavenly bodies, scientists will concede only that a statistical curiosity exists and nothing further.

In the Age of Aquarius we should pass through some period of uncertain length when there is a balance, a marriage of the yin/yang of magick and science, before we enter a reversed cycle. This will be a time when great gains are made in understanding; gains that bring us close to answering the "great questions".

For now, there is a great divide on the issue of manipulating physics with the mind. This is THE fundamental principle of magick. Witches believe that the laws of physics can be called into service to cooperate with our wishes when the request is made in the right way at the right time.

In this sense magick is about power. The great divide between maji-cians is over whether or not that power can be used to coerce, compel or manipulate others.

2. *Does Magick work?*

It's unlikely that anyone reading this book would ask this question, but, yes, it does. The real question is not, does it work?, but, rather, why does it work sometimes and not others? Or why is it unpredictable? Or why is there so much variance in results? Or why does the exact same spell work for one person and not another?

These are hard questions that shouldn't be avoided or denied. The truth is we don't know. The effects of magick may appear to be random at times. The odds are that, if we had the means to piece together an accurate picture with all factors and influences included, we would see that what appears to be random is quite logical and predictable. The fact that no one knows won't stop me from speculating or from indulging the vanity of calling the following an "educated guess".

Your magickal life is an extension of yourself; the whole package. That means the tapestry that seems to make sense when you're viewing it from the front (or finished) side and the back side as well, the part that we tend to forget about because it's hidden from view and makes no sense at all when you do look at it.

The end product of "you" is genetics plus the billions of bits of experi-ence that form your personal history.

*Your genetic make-up, that is, in the body you currently occupy.

*Your culture: not just your nationality or race, but the block on the street of the neighborhood of the town of the state of the country where you spent your formative years and were developmentally most influenced.

*The picture of your social journey; what adaptations did you impose upon your personality as a child and adolescent and what, if any, was your pay-off? Are there pivotal moments in memory that played a part in defining who you are now? What social concessions do you continue to make? What is your attitude toward friendship?

*What was the climate of your home life during your developmental years? What moments channeled your energies, or your interests, or your self-esteem this way or that?

*Were you liked by your teachers or generally unnoticed? Did you do well in school? Did you go to public or private school? Did you go to a private school with a religious agenda? What is the level and quality of your education?

*What was your socioeconomic status as a child and what is it now? What were your family's attitudes toward money?

*What is the culture of your career? Did you choose your occupation? Do you like your work? Is your work rewarding and satisfying or do you dread the very thought of Monday morning? Are you ambitious for material wealth or for recognition or both?

*What is your experience with sexuality? With romance? With relationships?

*What are your disappointments? Your failures? Your self-doubts?

All of these questions combined are just a sampling of those that could be asked about your surface, or apparent, personality. Even if you had the time, the means and the self-awareness to identify and factor into your magickal practice every building block of your personality, there would still be the gargantuan presence and influence of the subconscious mind. (The "you" that acts without the direction of your conscious self in dreams. The "you" that, for instance, surprises you with an erotic dream about a person who offers no attraction whatever to your conscious mind.) Add to that the possibility, perhaps even likelihood, of vestige memory or experience from past (or other) lives and the task is hopeless.

If all this wasn't daunting enough, such things as an undigested bit of grapefruit or the prolonged barking of a neighbor dog could create a shift in your ability to hold a magickal focus. This could mean that the attempt to replicate the precise same magickal thoughts and actions on another day could produce different results. Even if all conditions were identical, you, yourself, would be different.

You cannot cross the same magickal river twice because you and the river are both changed by the first crossing; if by nothing else.

There's also the question of intensity; how much you want it. In the spirit of continuing to build on the uncertainty, intensity can either attract or repel and it can be tricky to discern which will occur in a particular magickal circumstance. There are many "devil in the details" such oddities in the practice of magick, but, if it was easy, everyone would do it.

3. *How long does it take?*

The real question is- why isn't response immediate? Often it is. Some magickal activities, such as bindings, produce immediate results when done right. Magick you aim at another person at dawn can miss the other person altogether, but come round to bite you by dusk. Casting goals of a nonmaterial sort such as shifts in energy, consciousness, psychic ability and so on can be quick. Physical manifestations typically take longer. The length of time depends upon several things including your skill, the intensity of your desire and where the object would appear if we were to graph your sphere of influence.

Some things cannot be manifested immediately no matter who you are. I used to instruct my metaphysical students that a delay between the magnetizing of your desire and its physical manifestation is a good thing; a safeguard limitation of such sophistication as to suggest design – probably for protection of self and others. Until we can come to a better understanding of how the subconscious mind works, we must be protected from ourselves. Without this supervision, we might very well manifest whatever came to mind – elephants in the supermarket. If everyone's thoughts instantly sprang into being, the whole of creation could be undone in a day.

That some things cannot be manifested immediately no matter who you are is a fact of magick no matter how disappointing that might seem. The magickal world cannot be prodded, bribed or rushed. I'm not even certain that time, by our standard, is understood by the powers that assist in magickal affairs. If so, it is a dramatically different perspective. Even when we would desperately like an exception to this principle, it persists.

This year we began printing *Seasons* overseas for the first time; not so much for economic reasons, but because there were objections to "subject matter" by the U.S. printers we had used in the past. Most of the line arrived on schedule, but there were big problems with delivery of the day planners. The printer shipped three weeks later than promised. Then a typhoon in the South China Sea caused a change of ship and port. The container which was supposed to arrive the Port of Houston went to the Port of Los Angeles instead. New customs regulations pertaining to x-ray of imported goods held the books hostage for weeks instead of days. Customer patience was being put to the test. A couple of people asked why we didn't just cast a spell. The reason is simple …. because, even with a month's delay, the books would be here long before the results of a spell.

4. *Sphere of influence.*

The principle of Sphere of Influence is critical to magickal thinking. Metaphysicians refer to this principle as rate of vibration. In its most simplistic terms, it is how your mind acts to determine your present place in the world; socially and economically. This is what you are *in fact* and does not allow for any self-deception. If you change your circumstances without also changing your rate of vibration, the change will be temporary. The outward evidence, or material extension, of your thoughts will revert to the former state. Prime examples of this can be found in lottery winners who, within a short time of becoming millionaires, are back exactly where they were before.

In other words, perhaps you see yourself in a multimillion dollar, Malibu beach house, but, if you presently live in a mid-rent apartment, the place with the heavenly price tag exists far outside your Sphere of Influence.

You can acquire it magickally, but part of the price is time.

Just as you would use *Seasons of the Witch* as an aid to boost your magickal results, you can devise a mundane campaign to alter your Sphere of Influence. Your Sphere of Influence is like an invisible pond in which you will always occupy the center. If you take a step in any direction, there will be two effects. First, the movement will create ripples that extend to the outer edges and disturb the former stasis. (This is good because water in stasis becomes stagnant water.) Second, the sphere will adjust its radius in any direction you move so that you remain at the center.[1] If you are successful, this could dramatically reduce the time it will take to manifest your goal.

5. *Magick and Morality*

The Wiccan principle of "harm none", a small part of the Rede, pretty much seems to cover it. Every code of conduct since Hammurabi's Laws could be reduced to this simple theme. I do decry spells intended to harm not purely on moral grounds, but also because they are self-sabotage. You can't hide from cosmic justice and payback really is hell. Yes. Dark spells can be tempting, but my advice is this. Unless you're a masochist, don't do it.

Some spells are called negative, but are not negative in the sense of wickedness. Spells that banish or forbid trespass are spells of protection. Shooing away and limiting access is not causing harm. Spells that shame simply hold up a mirror. Spells that bind could be thought of as a kindness because, in a sense, you are saving the individual from her/himself if it was their purpose to do harm. Turning a person's negative energy

[1] I recently heard an elderly woman talk about how marvelous it is to visit with people she hasn't seen for decades and find that they are just the same, unchanged in any way except age. I nodded in agreement with a polite lie as she would not be able to process my perspective which is this. Nothing could be sadder than an individual who does not change in evident ways over a period of decades. If growth has been so miniscule that it could go undetected, to me that is a waste of life.

inward is not initiating harm, but rather containing it so that it doesn't contaminate others. Spells that repel are likewise protection spells. If you repel negative energy with no wish or intent for that energy to harm anyone else, there is, to my knowledge, no potential fallout from spells of repelling.

Chapter 2 Seven Kinds of Magick

What is NOT referenced on this list…

Mystery Schools. While Mystery Schools would usually be included in any listing of occult sciences, I will not include this form of magick here because the scope is apart from the basic premise of *Seasons*. As a brief definition, magickal systems such as Enochian, Qabalah, Hermetic, etc. are branches of magick sometimes called Mystery Schools. They are also known in some circles as "high magick"[1], a title no doubt bestowed by a disciple. These systems are more intellectual than intuitive. The goal is to attain magickal mastery and insight by study.

Black Magick. What is negative magick? Like the old saying regarding pornography, it is hard to define, but I know it when I see it. For one thing, there is absence of light. Magicks that use representations of persons, like poppets, are typically negative. Magicks with a goal of manipulating or compelling the will of another person are negative. Magicks used to conjure extra-normal assistance for the purpose of accumulating power over others are negative. And so on. And so on.

This is not a reference to a healthy understanding of the balance of light and shadow, but rather to persons whose spirits do not know or seek light. When encountering someone who aspires to a magickal practice, the first question is usually one of motivation. People are attracted to a deliberate practice of magick because they want more control or power over the world in which they live. Beyond this basic premise, which is true about each and every person who seeks the "Art", there is always a secondary motivation which is the key to predicting where this individual will gravitate within the circle of magickal choice.

[1] When the term "high magick" appears in *Seasons*, it is to reference an occasion when one might undertake a more elaborate working, one invested with planning, effort, formality and usually more drama as well.

People are attracted to dark magicks for one of three reasons. They're mad as hell (often at Christians). They want it quick and easy. Their damage is immutable.

a.)   Mad as hell. Those who come to magick because they're mad as hell are often that way because they find out they've been scammed by lies and the Christians who tell them; that Christianity was conceived as an aristocratic device for controlling underclasses, BIG business and subject to reinvention in every age. Easy to understand an anger reaction. Those who opt for Satan cults as a vehicle for protest, or revenge, must be dismissed as simpletons who haven't figured out that Satanists ARE Christians. The rest of us don't believe in a Devil per se and understand that this was just another Christianity malignation of pagan sacred beliefs; like a mud-slinging political campaign.

b.)   It probably didn't escape your notice that the framework of Star Wars is classically archetypal. That's because the great Joseph Conrad helped George Lucas with the outline. In the second film, technically known as Episode V, Luke Skywalker turns to Yoda and asks if the "dark side" is more powerful. Yoda replies that it is not more powerful, but that it is quicker, easier, more seductive. It is *not* more powerful, *not* quicker, *not* easier, but definitely more seductive. The appeal of the "dark side" is in the false promise of quick and easy. If it seems more effective, that is because of the belief invested by adherents.

c.)   After many years of reviewing and contemplating a host of perspectives on the subject of unredeemable evil, I have to go with this one. There are, in every generation, those who are here for one last chance to move in the direction of wisdom. If they fail, they will, upon the death of the body, fall through the lower realms until they are swallowed by the void, a bottomless pit where consciousness and experience ceases to exist. It is as if they never existed. In one sense that is regrettable. In another it is not.

What IS referenced...

Seven kinds of magick are referenced in *Seasons*. Most magickal practices are not limited to one of these, but are a combination. That selective use is typically known as "eclectic".

1. Tribal
Tribal magick is practiced by a culture at large and may or may not be with the specific knowledge or intent of tribe members. It is magick by osmosis. In American culture, this might include such things as:

a. childhood sayings – "I'm rubber and you're glue. What you say bounces off me and sticks on you." This is actually a perfectly written spell that needs nothing more than to be spoken three times.

b. Logos – Company logos are magickal glyphs. They are the essence of the company reduced to symbolic form.

c. tall buildings – Although the erection of taller buildings was first identified as negative magickal practice by Eastern mystics, it is no less true anywhere tall buildings exist. In modern times, higher is more powerful. The view is not the only reason penthouses never stay vacant long.

2. Crude and folk.

a. CRUDE - Practical magick is similar to number one, but is fueled by both knowledge and intent. The child who repeats the saying about rubber and glue is casting a spell that lacks full power because it is not fueled by intent. Practical magick includes acts of magickal heritage, sometimes called superstition, such as throwing salt over a shoulder, knocking on wood or refusing to walk under a ladder along with chants of magickal heritage which would be the repetition of sayings from the magickal heritage.

b. FOLK – Folk magick is one of the witchcraft paths that is a "calling". Witches who practice one or more of these forms are cousins to shamans and often demonstrate innate talents in this area. This path often combines elements of crude magick, but adds herbal (or kitchen) witchery; wildcrafting, wildgathering, cooking and healing with herbs, oils and plants. Witches who practice folk magick are inextricably tied to nature. They assume spirit in all things and are committed to protect that which sustains us.

Folk magick is the main reason witchery is called a craft. It is part art and part science. These are the descendents of those called Wise Ones.

3. Social

This is magick performed as a group (or coven) or with more than one person present. Social magick is thought to be more powerful because of collective purpose and power, but the basis for this belief seems to spring mostly from literary fiction. There are many excellent reasons why pagans should gather together: to celebrate sabbats or esbats, rites of passage, for information exchange and education, or just because it feels good to be amidst the like-minded.

While I believe that group magick is possible in theory, I also believe the odds against success grow exponentially with each person added. The reason is simple. Using the example of a personal portrait in photo form, you make an appointment with a photographer and call it a portrait. The photographer will probably give you instructions ahead of time about whether to wear a light or dark colors, high or low necklines, etc. Additionally you will take care with your personal grooming and will spend some measure of time picturing what the photo session will be like. With all this preparation mentally and physically it should only take one shot. Right? Regardless of whether or not it should take only one shot, the photographer is going to take many shots from several angles. Of those many shots s/he will choose a few and call them proofs. If you're lucky, you may be satisfied with one of those and call the effort a success. Sometimes the subject doesn't like any of the results.

As hard as it is to get a good portrait of one person, imagine how much more difficult it becomes if you want a family portrait. It gets harder to get good results with every person added. At some point, probably around the number seven, it becomes impossible. Even if every member of a group believes s/he shares the groups' motives and intentions, each member is processing reality through the filter of his/her experience, needs and desires. Add to that the crucial factor of focus and concentration. Even a group of adepts or elders will not mirror each others abilities. If you are working alone and you catch yourself thinking about the grocery list or a comment made by an acquaintance instead of what you're doing, you can start over until you get through your working without a lapse in concentration. There is a time for gathering and a time for solitude. My contention is that, when the occasion calls for being serious about the results of your working, you're better off working alone.

4. Pantheonic
Pantheonic magick is characterized by service to a deity or group of deities, such as that practiced by Children of Odin, or by service to aspects of nature such as that practiced by Druids. Pantheonic magick includes the channeling of deities or archetypes.

5. Solitary
Blessed be a solitary witch. Solitary witches are often self-initiated if at all. Their practice is often eclectic in that they use what works for them regardless of the source. This is surely the oldest of all paths. It is the path of wizards and sorcrerors in pursuit of genuine magick. It is the reclusive witch that figures prominently in literature from biblical to fairy tales. Solitaries are thoughtful, comfortable alone, and answer to no one but themselves. This is not to say that they aren't competent socially. They are often fun, witty and entertaining in social situations.

6. Elemental
I mention this not because it is a traditional "path" by definition, but because I reference it often in *Seasons of the Witch* and because the magickal approach is unique. This is magick that depends upon interaction with nonhuman creatures who are thought to have strong ties to the ancient elements. Some of these would include faeries, dragons, elves, gnomes, sylphs, salamanders, etc. Former humans are not part of this group. Neither are demons that have been created by belief and evocation.

Elementals are not physically bound to Earth as we are. Some are able to come and go between this dimension and others at will. Some must be summoned (or sent) with particular magicks. The reason they figure prominently in the collective consciousness of the race is because, in the not distant past, they spent much more time on this plane.

Sightings, and even interactions, were commonplace in certain parts of the world. As human population grew they came to feel less welcome here, for very good reason, or less comfortable because of large scale destruction of places where they felt most at home such as forests. Their main dwelling place is a plane of existence I call the Middle Kingdom.

I refer to opportunities for Elemental Magick in *Seasons* because this is, in my experience, an extremely powerful form of the Art. Little in life is as satisfying as alliances made with elementals as individuals or groups.

7. Divinatory

Divining is a magickal act which is why it's included here. *Seasons* notations normally refer to opportunities for spell casting. This is one of the exceptions in the sense that it refers to a spell opportunity as well as an opportunity to perform a specific action. *(For a complete list, See Non-Spell Activity, Chapter 12.)*

When special energy for divination presents itself, the occasion is marked. A spell cast over a session intended to divine information by magickal means will improve your results. The same spell cast during prime hours for divination should improve your results dramatically.

Chapter 3 The Path

What's a nice person like you doing on a path like this?

The first 7th House logo was not a glyph, but one of my paintings which I thought accurately represented the spirit of 7th House. It's the one I named "The Lady and The Wolf". It's about a nice girl who stepped off the road traveled by the many to take up company with the forest and the wolf. Childhood stories of being gobbled up by the wolf hadn't frightened her as they were intended to do. Along the way, she found the path that was true.

THE COMPANY OF WOLVES

How do you know you're a witch?

Many years ago I saw an actual self-test intended to determine the answer to this question. I've long since forgotten the source, but I can't imagine designing a test that could render accurate results.

The short answer is - you are if you think you are, provided that you're mature enough to be accountable for the choice and to make it for the right reasons.

You may be an hereditary[1] or you may be a Witch by choice. Regardless of attitudes held by some, points are not awarded for being born into a particular family group. The choice to walk a pagan path is credential in itself and demonstrates traits of courage and character not required by those born into the Craft. Some people are not hereditaries in the ancestral sense, but have magickal or psychic skills acquired in past lives. Some people are hereditaries and don't know it because family elders were underground Pagans or Witches. This would be particularly true in areas where there was strong communal intolerance for individuality. Clues to this past may be found in the discovery that family members were Masons or Eastern Star. Look at grandparents and their grandparents. Innate talents in the Arts often skip a generation. If you are especially curious, you can also pose the question outright on Samhain night to any discarnate who shares your blood.

The Hereditary Query Ritual:

This is a solitary ritual to be conducted on Samhain night after the trick-or-treaters have come and gone, but before midnight. Here are some elements you might include in your celebration.

1.   A sealed circle of salt and a strong protection spell. As you are pouring the salt in a circle, speak words to the effect that all within must vacate before the circle is complete[2] and all without must remain without until called. After you are safely sealed inside the circle, use your inner eye to set the salt on fire. The image is of blue flames rising high and forming a circular, barrier shield.

[1] A person who descends from a line of witches and has learned the Craft directly from a member of this descent or who has inherited traits embedded in genetic memory from an ancestor.
[2] Make certain you are understood *clearly*, no matter how painstaking the process, because some Elementals are very smart and some are quite the opposite. You're the witch and that makes you responsible for the ones who are dumb.

2.   The burning of dry grass to honor your ancestors who had no knowledge of the magickal arts. The burning of Solomon's Seal (coupled with one of the psychic booster herbs or oils[3]) as an offering to your ancestors who have specific knowledge on this subject; either they were witches themselves or they knew others who were. The aroma of the burning herb will help you move toward a place of receptivity.

3. An invitation to revelation for those spirits who: (a.) know what you seek to know, (b.) are willing to share with you (c.) are motivated by your best interest and (d.) would be willing to support you or guide you in your practice . This caution added because people don't suddenly become wise or good by simply moving away from their bodies.

4. Use a self-guided meditation to reach out with your feelings, but DO NOT go to them. Let them come to you. This is not the best time to go for a walkabout in the Astral regions.

5. Vow that you will trust that the images, words or phrases that come to you are messages that you will commit to heart until such time as the meanings become clear. You can also ask for clarification in dreams.

6. Thank those who have chosen to commune with you and bid them go in peace even if your skill level is not at a stage where you feel sure anyone else is present. Better to err on the positive side.

Signs

Children with natural talents for magick often reveal a proclivity early and in various ways. Unfortunately, they are rarely born into families prepared to recognize what they're witnessing, much less honor it. My mother says certain people felt uncomfortable around me from a very early age; that I had a piercing gaze that made some feel like their souls were being examined. She says one woman was visiting when I had just learned to pull up and stand holding onto the sides of a playpen. The woman began to appear distracted and unable to concentrate on the

---

[3] See the chapter on Psychic Herbs in *The Master Grimoire* by Pat Kirven Sawyer.

conversation. Finally, she asked my mother, "Does that baby look at everyone that way?" She was the first of many grown-ups who would be conspicuously uneasy in my presence when I was a child. It's especially regrettable that some of those were teachers.

A child with "night terrors" may be an example of demonstrating sorcery in infancy. In social situations I enjoy asking people about their earliest memories. I have rarely shared mine, but here it is. I was two-years-old and still sleeping in a bed with rails in my parents bedroom. My bed was by the closed-in porch on the edge of the forest. I think it was likely a forrested hillside lot that was vacant, but it seemed magickal to me. I woke in what may have been a sense of anticipation--something coming, pulled myself to a standing position and looked to see that my parents were sleeping. In a moment or two I was visited by something that would bedifficult to describe. For purposes of brevity, let's say it was abnormally tall and bearish. I wasn't the least frightened because I had no context for suspecting this might be out of the ordinary. So far as I knew, at that age, this was an everyday occurrence. The thing looked at me for a couple of minutes, then turned and silently left the way it came.

I would not again see such a thing with my physical eyes for another forty years. In the in-between my only gauge for knowing when something extraordinary was present was an awareness of a shift in the atmosphere.

> *all the angels, all the devils,*
> *all around us, can't you see?*
> > - Sting

After I started school I absorbed from the culture what is acceptable ("normal") and what is not. There were only two cultural reference points for extra-dimensional presence. One was angels, the other ghosts/monsters. Since the horror genre has a much bigger impact on the psyche, I came to believe that something "else" meant scary. This is a pattern that seems fairly common among such children. When I would wake in the night and sense that I was not alone in my room, I would run to my parents' bedside for refuge. Many children who find themselves outside culturally sanctioned experience report bad dreams because no other vernacular is available.

As a child I demonstrated signs that I was born with an ability to probe people's hearts and work with extra-dimensional species. You came with gifts, too. Do you know what they are? Watch for signs in the children who are close to you. Unusual gifts are marvelous, but lonely. You might be the only voice of comfort, encouragement or comradery.

The Broom Closet

With a few exceptions, most of our customers feel like they live in *the* most Pagan-hostile place in the world. Few are openly Pagan in every part of their lives. Some are open to family, but not at work. Others are open only to coven members. Many who are partnered seem to be partnered with persons who have other beliefs. Some of these are tolerant and some are clearly charmed by their partner's persuasions and seem almost proud that their lovers are Witches. Every Yule season there is a last-minute flurry of calls from husbands and boyfriends who are giving *Seasons* as a gift. It pleases us to know that many of our customers are so well-matched.

A couple of times people have returned books against their will because their presence caused "trouble in the household". I sympathize with these individuals' needs to learn their own lessons in their own time, but suspect that their days spent in the household of someone so spiritually foreign and overbearing are numbered. No lasting happiness can come from a partnership in which one dictates what the other will practice and believe.

Chapter 4 Astrology +

The role of weather in magick.

You're already aware of the powerful influence of heavenly bodies on your practice of magick or you wouldn't be reading this book. Closer to home, elements dance to the movements of our own planet. I have found that witches are often sensitive to weather. Perhaps because they tend to be more conscious that we are part of, and not separate from, nature. I think weather is vital to spellwork both in terms of matching current climate to type of spell and in terms of what excites us or deters us. For example, it's just darn hard to be excited about candle magick when the weather is hot. Knowing that lighting those candles is going to heat up your interior space even more can muster up a good deal of dread. On the other hand, it is exciting to light candles when the weather is cool. It adds warmth, atmosphere and magick. That's a win times three.

There's no escaping the fact that certain kinds of spells lend themselves to certain kinds of weather. Even entire systems have clustered in geographical regions along climatic lines. For example, the largest body of work in the area of sex magick originates in places that are hot and humid. What we know about fire magick comes largely from places where there are many more cold days than warm.

The lesson here is the same as in the principle behind *Seasons of the Witch* power days. It's easier to cast with the flow. Windy days are wonderful days for air magick. Rainy days are wonderful days for water magick. Cold days are wonderful days for fire magick. And so on. If you ever find yourself dreading an aspect of a spell or work with a particular magick, don't bother. You're not going to get anywhere using the thing that seems daunting or like a chore.

If something about the weather seems magickally exciting, pay attention and act on that calling. Lots of witches find electrical storms irresistible, the more thunder the better. If you find yourself tingling with the sounds of a surprise storm, take advantage of the situation. If nothing else, go to the window and spend a minute *connnecting* with the energy.

Time of Day

Timing can be a powerful tool in itself. Your analytical side knows that the Earth circles the Sun. Still there is an emotional you, a romantic, poetic you, who thinks in terms of sunrises and sunsets as if these were descriptions of actual events. The analytical part of your brain isn't really welcome at the magick circle because it just doesn't belong. You may be a math teacher by profession, but you can't add two and two when you're asleep and dreaming. In your dream state you may know that you can do math, but your ability stops there. No matter how hard you strain, you can't add in dreams. The same is true of spelling. The part of you that dreams doesn't accept analytical, arbitrary symbols and has no use for them. It's that part, the non-analytical part, that works magick.

If it works out that you're doing a spell that involves "beginnings" and power energy is available early in the morning, the sunrise can be a tool that enhances the notion of beginning. Likewise, sunset could be an excellent time for an "amicable parting" spell.

Most timing is magickal common sense. Clearing spells, clarity spells, resolve quarrels spells are best done in bright sunny conditions when possible. Most magick, however, is best performed after dark. That's why I would vote against daylight savings if given the chance.

Magick and Your Chart

Naturally your personal astrological influences factor into your spellwork results. At simplest level, if you are a Pisces sun sign, for example, you will probably find scrying with mirrors child's play. On the other hand, spells that require fire energy may require a lot of extra effort and perhaps staging such as surrounding yourself with literal fire (candles). The success of your practice depends upon identification of participating factors and giving them weight. There are always compensatory measures. The balance required for successful magick is always an achievable goal when you know what you're dealing with and allow for it.

The Elemental Personality

If you are working with elements, and all witches must at some time or another, watch out for how the elements are represented in your personality and be aware that each has an effect.

Every one of us has all four ancient elements represented within us, but how much of each is partly attributable to astrology and partly due to genetics. It's a good idea to consider your elemental leanings and how they can affect your spells. Arrange the four ancient elements as they appear in your personality from most to least. For example...

1. air   2. earth   3. fire   4. water

This person should be in a calm place when approaching elemental spells because air is the one element that has power over the other three, including the power to excite and even anger.

Explore how your unique mix of elements might effect your magick for good or bad.

SECTION I MY THEORY OF MAGICK

Chapter 5 Know Thyself

This is the key. Your intuition may be tuned to "buzz" you when it's time to perform a particular magick like an alarm clock. Your astrological influences, your personality type, your psychological history, your education (religious and secular) all play a part in what you brings to the altar for a particular purpose at a particular time.

Magick and Personality

If we were to try to identify where magick resides in psychological terms, we would say it originates in the subconscious mind. The subconscious mind is home to your magickal mind. The magickal mind is without sophistication, cultural layerings and mores. The magickal mind cannot write a diplomatic sentence, but the magickal mind comes closer to knowing your true desires than any part of you.

I discovered an aspect of this principle many years ago at a psychic fair. I sat down in front of a dowser who was working with a crystal pendulum. He said that he would begin by establishing directional swings with yes and no questions. He swung the pendulum north/south and said, "This is yes." Then east/west, "This is no." He asked my name. I gave it. The pendulum swung east/west for "no". I laughed and said, "That is my name." I repeated it. The pendulum swung further east/west. The dowser asked me if I was sure about my name. At that point I began to doubt his credibility. I asked the pendulum to accept my nom de plume. It said no. I asked the pendulum to accept my magickal name. It said no. Then, as a last resort, I asked the pendulum to accept my name exactly as it appears on my birth certificate, the pendulum swung happily, yes, yes, yes. So far as my magickal mind is concerned, the name I was given at birth is my name. Period.

The experience made a big impression on me. After that I always felt like I was fibbing when I gave my married name. A few years later I had my name legally changed back to my "real" (maiden) name to please my magickal mind.

In social science terms it has been said that this part of you, the subconscious mind, is the vast iceberg that floats beneath the surface of a small, visible peak represented by the conscious mind. In magick we seek to gain a small bit of cooperation from that part of ourselves.

Self-Awareness as Magickal Anchor

Every year there are power opportunities for self-reflection and/or assessment. My sense is that these are usually ignored because they are not as exciting or sexy as things such as wealth and power. If I'm right about that, then it is a shame because self-awareness is magick's anchor. If you don't know who you are and where you are both in relation to the world in general and in relation to where you want to be, you have no starting point, no frame of reference. Going for the glam without paying dues is an immature approach to a magickal practice that will render what one might expect. You do get what you pay for.

Maybe that little bit of hunger is a need for more money, but, if it's something else, more money won't quench that tickling of unknown desire. Before you expend the energy required to cast a solid spell, invest some effort to determine what you really want. This is part of preparation. Do the homework.

Magickal Talent - Natural and Learned

One of the great divides in the community of the magickal Arts regards natural ability versus learned ability. To me it's like the conversation between a person who has encountered an apparition of a discarnate spirit and another who has not. The one who has not seen a ghost will typically adopt a posture of skepticism coupled with an unmistakable air of superiority (usually conveyed by a self-satisfied smirk). The person whose experience causes them to step outside the safe body of conventional knowledge makes her/himself vulnerable to the jibes and sneers of those who are less fortunate because of a more limited view of reality.

There may be some gender advantages when it comes to natural ability. Expressions such as "women's intuition" are usually met with nods of shared belief. In the past twenty years science has found differences in the brains of men and women both in terms of equipment and chemistry that may someday explain what we all know to be true. Still, I think all people have intuitive ability. It's just more macho when it's called a "hunch" or "gut feel".

In the late seventies I was invited to a small social gathering at the home of a friend. The purpose of the get-together was partly "girls night out" and partly to meet a guest always referred to by my friend as her psychic. Iris, the psychic, was a Cajun visiting from Louisiana for the weekend. She was handsome and uncommercial, probably forty, with glasses and long, straight dark hair. She had one of those envious complexions dark enough to glow through the winter with no sun. Like many people of the time her beauty regimen consisted of "a wash and a brush".

We sat in the living room, some on the floor pillows, drank some Chablis, told stories and laughed together while candles flickered. On several occasions I caught the "psychic" staring at me out of the corner of my eye. When I would turn to face her, she didn't look away as most people would. She just smiled and continued to stare until I looked away.

After some time, when things got quiet, she said, "I can see Victoria has way too much stress held between her shoulder blades." She bade me come and sit in front of her on the floor with a promise that she would release some of that tension. People shifted positions to make room for me so that I could sit cross-legged on the floor in front of the guest of honor who was on the sofa. She placed her palm flat on my back between my shoulder blades and left it there. After a minute or so the area began to feel warm. She told me to close my eyes. I did. To the best of my recollection I think I saw myself on the other side of a tunnel, the sort you would encounter just west of Denver on I70 where you could stop in the middle and see light at either end. The next time Iris spoke to me she sounded far, far away, muffled, like she was on the other side of a wall.

I was confused, but not frightened or concerned. On the one hand I knew that I was just inches away from the person speaking. On the other hand I was somewhere else. Finally, I said, "Where are you?"

My friend had invited people of all ages to this gathering. One of the guests had brought a daughter who was about fifteen. She was too young to understand that something remarkable was happening. She found my question very amusing and laughed out loud. The laughter jolted me back to my body because, apparently, I was more afraid of being the butt of a joke than I was curious about where the experience would lead.

This is how I came to know that I was born with a talent for astral travel. Of course, I didn't know that's what it was at the time. For a couple of years thereafter I went to lengths to avoid it. I found it disconcerting, more a bother than anything else because it caused me to curtail some favorite activities. I found that if I got still in a warm bath and closed my eyes, I was gone. If I embarked upon a meditation, I was gone. I had no control and no idea what was happening.

Eventually I gained the courage to fly deliberately. The witch (for today she would not be hiding behind the term "psychic" and would be called truly) released my power of flight. I don't know how she knew it was there or how she did it. I don't know if it is an acquired skill brought forward from another lifetime. I just know that I have it and I didn't have to work for it as I must for other things.

The point of this story is to say that you may very well have one or more magickal gifts that are dormant, waiting to be awakened by some happy accident or another. Even if you don't have one of the glamorous talents, you can develop your intuition so that it works as well as your other five senses.

Chapter 6 Spell Casting

The first step is identifying a need. The second step is making a decision to cast a spell. The third step is deciding what kind of spell to cast. Your spell begins with the planning. The pressure builds until it bursts in climax at the moment you pronounce the magickal lightning strike in mid spell.

1.) Identifying a need. One day something niggles at you. You know you're not hungry, but you don't feel full either. There's something missing. You get a flash that says, "Hey! I need a boyfriend, or a promotion, or a new house, or a vacation," etc. etc. etc. You're alive!

2.) Making a decision to cast. Once you have settled on a thing or essence you would like to draw to you, you make a decision that you will cast a spell. I love the term casting. It brings up images of throwing a magickal net by moonlight across the sparkling sea of the cosmos knowing that it contains what you want.

3.) *What kind of spell will it be?*

      a. The first thing I would do is go to *Seasons of the Witch* to locate the next day with power energy relating to the thing I need.

      b. The next thing I would do is decide the intensity needed to bring me this thing. *(*Refer to *Sphere of Influence* in Chapter 1.*)* This can seem like a moving target. Spell intensity can fall anywhere along a continuum from a quick wish murmured under your breath to a full scale dramatic production that takes weeks or months to mount and weeks or months to recover from. Ideally you want to choose to come close to the amount of energy necessary.

Guidelines are hard because this is very subjective. If you want the thing really, really badly (can't live without it) and it's pretty far outside your Sphere of Influence, then you need to put everything into it. Even with a big bang spell, manifesting may take quite awhile because you have to expand and move your Sphere of Influence along with calling this thing to you. You have to put a lot in to get a lot out.

If you want the thing badly (you could live without it if you have to), then you need to approach the spell with sincerity, plan ahead for at least three weeks and get out all your best magickal stuff, but hold enough of your energy back so that you could go to work the next day.

And so on until you form this equation. $(A1-A2) + B = C$

A1 = The magickal proximity of the thing you want
A2 = Your current situation.
B = The intensity of your desire
C = The appropriate intensity of the spell.

If the spell is worth performing, it's worth doing well.

4.) *The Casting Check List*

The check list is based on the idea of eliminating what may go wrong when you can. Many of the items mentioned here will be addressed in more detail further on.

If you are serious about a successful practice, you must keep meticulous notes. A Book of Shadows and Light is a good place for keeping such records, but any sort of journal or notebook will do. Approach this task with precision. Think of yourself as a mystic conducting a scientific experiment. Record every detail about the experience no matter how small. If you notice it, write it down. You may find that the required level of self-awareness is an exercise that indirectly hones your intuition skills. The following checklist would apply to solitary spellwork. These would include, but not be limited to the following.

-        Day, Month, Year

-        Time of Day

-        The moon is ruled by what astrological sign?

- What is the subject and purpose of the spell? Be detailed about your goals.

- Is this within the time frame for major or minor power as per tains to spells for this purpose?

- Are you alone? If not, who is with you? Are they part of your working or just on the premises?

- What is the weather like?

- Is it light or dark outside? (Time of day may not always convey this information.)

- How are you dressed?

- What is your mood?

- How do you feel about your ability to concentrate?

- When did you last eat and what was it?

- Have you done anything special to prepare your body to house the priest(ess) that you will be during spellwork? For example, when and how did you last bathe? What products did you use?

- Are you experiencing any physical distractions such as sore muscles, allergies, arthritis, etc?

- Are you in time of transition such as relocation, change of jobs, courtship, marriage, divorce, etc.?

- Are you casting outside or inside?

- Where are you? Record the details of your surroundings. (If this is a place where you have or will cast on repeated occasions, you only need to record great detail once. Thereafter, you can just mention changes. The first time you enter this information it should be refined right down to colors and materials used in structure. Also mention whether the space is messy or neat, clean or not so clean.

- Are you on the ground or on the ground level of a building? Or are you on a higher story?

- What sounds may effect your concentration? Are there intermittent bird noises? Does the heat/cool come on and off? (After ward, be sure to add any noises that you recall that were not anticipated such as a dog barking, a phone ringing, a neighbor starting a motorcycle, etc. and at what point in the spell progression this occurred.)

- Are you using sound, such as a CD or tone chime, as part of your spellwork?

- Of what smells are you aware? (My good friend who is a master aromatherapist first taught me that smells create a sense memory that generates very powerful emotional associations.) Some of your tools may have memorable odors: incense, herbs, oils and candles. Also, are you wearing a scent? If so, is it synthetic or made of essential oils? Did you bathe in a scented oil?

- If you are a woman in the years of menses, where are you in your cycle? If you are aware of other reproductive or hormonal variants that could have an effect, write it down.

- Are you working with a spell that is completely your creation, one that you have modified or one that was written by someone else?

- On what date did you first decide that you were casting on this day?

- What tools are you using? Be specific. If you're using tarot, name the cards and the deck. If you're using candles, say what color, what size, how many, whether they were scented or not and, if so, with what? If there was anything special, such as beeswax candles, write it down. (herbs, oils, athame, crystals, incense, blessed water, flowers, statuary, etc.) Mention anything that is unusual for you such as a new tool or an unfamiliar incense. Also, mention relevant specifics. For instance, if you are deliberately using pure sea salt as opposed to Mortons, it's worthy of note.

- What steps have you taken to prepare your tools, if any?

- Draw a diagram of what you are placing where.

- Write out the steps of the spell including when you will be sitting and when you will be standing or moving. Make note of what things you say or sing out loud and what is repeated silently.

If you think all this sounds too complicated, the practice of magick may not be right for you. On the other hand, over time your diligence may pay off with the emergence of patterns that can be invaluable. For example, you may find you have more success with wealth spells in cold weather. You may find astral travel is easier for you when it's dark or when you're in a bath of salt water or when you first wake in the morning or when no one else is at home.

Cast a spell on yourself to compel yourself to recognize your results when they manifest. Sometimes results come after you stop listening for the knock on the door. Sometimes they come in a form unlike what you saw in your mind when you cast, but as the essence of a thing and often as a version better than you requested. When you realize that your spell has come to fruition, go back and close the notation with the result being the last entry.

SECTION I MY THEORY OF MAGICK

SECTION II

What You Need

SECTION II WHAT YOU NEED

Chapter 7 Mindset

Belief

The single most important thing about your practice of witchcraft is belief in your ability to persuade the laws of physics and destiny to reorganize reality in your image. You are morally free to use any means necessary to accomplish this provided that you are the only one effected by your choices. I agree wholeheartedly with the chaos magician, Pete Carroll, on the issue of borrowing imagery or substance from any source that you find useful: movies, books, posters, anything.

Here's an example. I came across a small wooden statue of Yoda at a market years ago. I bought it for a child in the family, brought it home and put it on my bookshelf to wait until the occasion came round. Meanwhile, I came across the principle of infusing ordinary objects with magickal essences, principles or tasks. At the time I was faced with a dilemma. I decided to give Yoda the job of helping me sort things out. So he became "ask Yoda" and found a permanent home in my library. He's on staff in every sense except salary. If the choice is particularly perplexing he gets center stage in a circle for clarity spell. If a character or image from a fantasy source strikes you as magickal, then it is. When you're working alone, there's no such thing as silly.

Magickal Sense

Your magickal senses are simply your regular senses jumped up on witchy intuition. When I talk in these pages about seeing with your magickal eyes, for instance, it means looking to see the potential magick factor in a person, place or thing or, conversely, looking to see if there is a magickal inhibitor in a given person, place or thing. All of your senses are available to psychic upgrades. A little work in this area will render big rewards. There are power opportunities throughout each year for honing psychic skills. Using your senses magickally is one of the most practical of the magick Arts and one that is available to everybody.

Remember that the voice you hear will usually be your own[1]. Yes. It can be tricky to distinguish messages from the barrage of audio gibberish constant in contemporary life. You may follow some leads that go nowhere. But, if you stay receptive and pay attention, you'll be rewarded for your efforts. Look in your planner or calendar for power days identified as opportunities for intuition spells or psychic development spells.

[1]The voice you hear will be your own except at times when you literally hear another. I was out with my youngest daughter when she was in her early teens. During a break in the conversation I was walking along, looking at the sidewalk and thinking to myself, "Am I on the right path?" I had just spent some considerable time doing research of a mystical nature. She looked at me suddenly, smiled and said, "Don't worry, Mom. You're on the right path." It was one of those events that is shocking and thrilling at the same time. She kept walking.

Thinking it must have been some form of telepathy, I said, "In your mind did you hear me ask myself that question?"

"What question?" she asked.

She had no recollection of thinking or saying anything about a path. This was the first of several such exchanges with this daughter that have occurred over the years. Some power that wants to communicate with me uses her as a literal mouthpiece to send messages from time to time.

Of all my children this particular daughter is least interested in the magickal or mystical even though she may be magickally gifted herself and grow into it as she ages. (This was foretold by an incident when she was sixteen. One of her older sisters stopped suddenly in the sunlight and, to our amazement, pulled a long, white hair from her beautiful dark locks. It is the portent of a wise woman to-be. Prematurely white has long since been ruled out as she is well into adulthood now.)

The point of the story is that messages will normally come to you in a form that would not be heard by anyone else, delivered to your consciousness by a voice that sounds identical to the one you hear when you're reading. Unless it's otherwise.

Chapter 8 Magick Space

For me *where* is as important as what, who and how. If you are sensitive enough to be drawn to the practice of magick, you are probably extra-aware of your environment to begin with. I would go so far as to say that you should take certain principles into account when choosing a place to live. Whether buying or renting, don't move in until you look with your "magickal eyes". I'll mention a few factors you might take into consideration. Also, when at all possible I ask a friend with witchy intuition to go with me for a second opinion visit before signing contracts. Here are some sample questions you might ask. Most of them were learned the hard way.

Have the people who lived here before been happy? Is there any lingering residue of anger or pain that would be resistant to clearing?

It is my fortune, or misfortune depending upon your point of view, to have lived in a lot of different places in my adult life. Here is one of those stories.

The owners of a beautiful house were transferred to another city. They were unable to sell right away. So they leased the house. We were the second family to lease. Within a few weeks things seem to go off kilter. What ensued were problems with work, health and family members not getting along with each other. One day my intuition told me to look into the history of the house. I didn't have to look far. A little research gave up the story that the previous tenant had been going through a very dark time. He had failed at a business venture, he was on the verge of bankruptcy and was being hounded by creditors. In the midst of all this, his wife left him. After several months of not paying rent, he was evicted from the house. Even though this poor man had vacated physically, the feelings of desperation and hopelessness remained layered underneath the landlord's anger at being stiffed. This experience is the one that taught me to get a second opinion. I had been so caught up in the appeal of amenities that I had not allowed myself to receive warning signals emanating from the house. They surely were present. They always are.

Are there unseen entities of negative nature that would be resistant to clearing?

We moved to Houston in 1982 right at the end of the boom caused by the relocation of the big oil companies. Our plan was to lease a house for a year or so and then buy, but, because of the boom, there weren't a lot of choices. We ended up in the Amityville Horror.

The first night in the house I tossed and turned and finally gave up on sleep in the wee hours. I sat up for the rest of the night alternating between reading and doing visual house blessings. The bedrooms were all on the second floor of the house and, as it turned out, that in itself was a blessing. My side of the bed was situated so that, when sitting up, I could look down the hallway and see the doors to all the children's rooms. For the remainder of the time we spent in that house, about two years, I stayed awake while the rest of the family slept; sitting up in bed where I could see the doors to all the children's rooms. It was involuntary. Not a conscious decision at all. At the core of my magickal mind, I knew something was wrong with the house. Mercifully, my normal requirement for sleep, typically nine hours or so, was suspended for nearly two years. It sounds impossible, but it's true nonetheless.

In the first few weeks the children would sometimes report phenomena such as fans turning on and off by themselves. They weren't terrified by these occurrences, more curious really. The rest of the time we were in the house the children and my husband were able to go about their business blissfully oblivious. Oddly, the lack of sleep didn't show up in my looks, my health, my energy level, my focus or otherwise that I noticed.

Sometime after we moved in a neighbor who had lived there for years reported that "devil worshipers" had occupied the house before us. This particular neighbor was evangelical Christian. She had a recording that played from a front door speaker twenty-four hours a day. When you got halfway up the walk to her door you would begin to hear the sounds differentiate into hellfire and brimstone preaching. I had a polite acquaintance with this woman but, obviously, didn't put much stock in her opinions. I asked what made her think they were Satanists. She reported some unusual things to be sure, but nothing conclusive and went on to say that everyone in the neighborhood knew this. I don't believe in the Christian "Devil-god", but I do believe that people with belief, intention and tools can conjure things that resemble what they want to see. There's no way to say what went on in that house, but something dark had been called and not dismissed. I suspect the neighbor's recording was the result of her own sense that she needed an amulet of sorts.

Eventually we bought a brand new house. At the time I was too tired to deal with any more houses that came with history. We did one of those grueling, all day weekend moves. Finally, I thought we had made the last trip. With relief I was preparing to put my full weight down in my new house. Then we realized we had left a few odds and ends that would require one more trip to the other house about half an hour away.

I took my two oldest children with me. It was just getting dark when we opened the front door of that house for the last time. Like a whoosh I felt an unpleasant rush of chemicals and I knew instantly that whatever had claimed the house was back and angry about having been bound for so long. Just as instantly I knew that I must have, subconsciously, taken with me the energy I had used to keep the thing at bay. I thought had thought we were finished with the house and would not be back. The result was that of unlocking a cage. I decided that we would just run through, grab the stuff and get out quickly.

At first the kids were unaware, but gradually they began to feel it. It was the only time I have ever seen my children terrified. It's not an experience I recommend to any mom. My son, himself an archetype of masculine energy, was way too proud to be deterred from a task just because he was uncomfortable. He came to do a job and, by all the gods, he wasn't leaving without doing it. Eventually my daughter and I were both begging him to drop the wrench and leave the stuff. I remember how her voice was shaking. The car was very quiet on the way back to the new house. I slept through the night for the first time in two years.

Last, I strongly recommend that you visit the prospective residence at night as well as day because, as you know, sometimes there is a very large shift in energy after sunset.

Clearing the Space

First and foremost, PLEASE tell me you didn't move in without clearing the space first as I have done all too often. If you did, then, for gods'
sake, put this at the top of your priority list for your next day off. I use
the old, tried and true methods.

Light your pillar candles. Then light a nice bunch of tied white sage.
Encircle yourself in the smoke while you're creating some protections
around yourself. Open the main entry door and leave it standing open.
Start in the farthest part of the house with your smoking sage and begin
chanting a quatrain (preferably one composed by you) to rid the property
of anything unwanted, seen or unseen.

Work your way toward the front door room by room, herding everything
you don't want in that direction just the way you would round up live-
stock. Have a pot by the front door to put your sage in along with a dish
of salt. Put down the sage with a final 'hit the road' command. Sprinkle
your salt across the threshold and close the door with authority.

I also put little mirrors on my doors at eye level, to discourage wrongdo-
ers of the human sort. At the same time I cast a spell to the effect that
only people who have our best interest at heart will feel comfortable on
the premises. Others will simply not be able to stay. The downside is that
you may have a very hard time finding a handy man who will return for
repeated visits. The upside is that they won't come back if they're up to
no good.

Multihome and Multistory Dwellings.

Cast spells on the ground or on a ground floor if you can. I say this
partly from experience and partly because I intuit that there are too many
variables when vacuous spaces occur beneath you. If you are casting on a
floor or platform that is elevated above the earth and not filled in with

earth, there are vacuous spaces beneath you. Spells cast successfully may take flight, but they should originate on the ground.

If you live above the first floor in a flat, apartment or loft, the space is less than ideal for magick and not much can be done to correct that, but you can compensate in a couple of ways. Place the tools used in your spell, and altar if you keep one, on materials of the earth such as dirt, salt or sand. When you are preparing to cast, gather and arrange your tools in suitable position. When planning the circle or casting area, leave room for yourself to sit. Think of yourself as the primary tool, the only one that must be present.

Before you begin your spell, every time, seat yourself in your casting area, cross-legged if this position is comfortable for you. Close your eyes and visualize a teletransportation in which you move yourself and your entire circle, as if on magic carpet, to an appropriate setting. You can actually picture yourself and your casting area flying through the air and coming to rest in a place that attracts the majician in you. (See *What Kind of Witch Are You?* later in this chapter.) You may land on a mountaintop or by a mountain lake, on a deserted beach, in the desert or in a forest clearing. Use music if you find it helps you with self-guided visualizations. Once you have a firm image of your alter-location, surround it with a stiff security spell in the form of a shield that can only be penetrated by you. Then you can proceed with your spell.

If you are working with elementals or other entities, you can invite them into your magick space, but make sure they have been properly dismissed and are gone before you leave and seal the premises. This is not work for the careless or forgetful as you are responsible for what happens there. If there is a chance you may get caught up or distracted and leave an elemental trapped in a space of your creation, then ignore this passage and move on.

The first time you perform a teletransportation through magick space you should take your time and go slowly. Infuse the process with detail and emotion. Feel yourself lift off. Feel the air rush by on your journey. When you arrive at your alter-location, make adjustments to the surroundings until you decide it is perfect for your purpose. Adjust the light, the temperature, the sounds, the vegetation and the overall feel so that it is truly a magickal place to you. If you return to this same spot in the future the time it takes to place yourself and your things in magick space will be gradually reduced. If you return many times you will eventually program yourself to go there instantly and without much effort.

That is because magick space in the form of alter-location, when created by a witch, begins as an imaginary journey, but becomes a real place in a non-physical dimension. Every time the space is used it gains more substance, sort of like accruing matter. Eventually it could be accessed by elementals without invitation which is the main reason why you should make a habit of reestablishing firm security barriers when you're not there.

Your ideal space.

As I've said before, everything is important in the practice of magick. Everything in the space where you perform magick becomes part of the cauldron stew, even the color of the walls and the material in the big chair. This is because you are aware and registering perceptions of your surroundings even when you are not consciously thinking about them. Things such as the color of the rug or the fabric pattern in the pillows or, gods forbid, unfinished work on the laptop or a basket of laundry to be done. This is one of the reasons why a secure, unblemished outdoor location is most ideal; because the only factors are you, your tools, your clothes and nature. A lot of guesswork is taken out of the equation, but we all know that isn't practical or even possible for most people in urban areas. In fact, in the 21st century, it's difficult in most rural areas as well.

Soon after I began dabbling in the arts, I moved to a place that happened to be ideal for magick or close to it. My abilities seemed to expand exponentially day by day. It was like pulling the rip cord on an inflatable raft. I give this as an example of the role environment can play in magick.

The room I used for my magick practice was large. It sat on the north west side of the house and looked out across lawn toward a large stand of trees. The north wall was windowed without coverings as the view was private, with French doors in the center of the wall. It had white walls, a gray, polished flagstone floor and a large fireplace set at an angle in the northwest corner. Three large skylights were inset in the ceiling where you could see the stars by night and the leaves of towering trees by day. It was all the more magickal for me because it was also my art studio, a place of joy where I regularly pursued visions of fantasy and magick. Since the room had little furniture, no drapes, carpet or even wood floors, it rendered a beautiful echo with bright sound. There was also a built-in cabinet on the west side with a mirrored wall behind it. The cabinet just happened to be elevated to the perfect height for an altar. My tools were close at hand for magick, but hidden in the cabinet the rest of the time.

On cool nights I would light a fire and place votive candles in crystal bases around the perimeter of my circle. The crystal reflected the fire-light while the candlelight danced on the polished stone floor. The room seemed alive. (See *The Magick of Reflective Surfaces* in Chapter 12.) The fire's crackle was amplified by the acoustics as was the ringing of a hand chime I sometimes used when drawing a circle. Occasionally I would play a favorite McKennitt CD for inspiration to give my spell movement through dance. I used a copper pot to burn herbs, incense, chunks of Dragon's Blood resin and parchment notes. I would set the fire in the pot and spin it doesil[1] on the stone floor. The sound of the spinning echoing through the room gave rise to the power of the spell.

Occasionally I was treated to phenomena. A couple of times close to the dark of Yule, when working dragon magick, the doors, which had been firmly secured by latch sliding into the floor on bottom and into the door facing on top, burst open in the middle of a spell. The display was delightful beyond words.

It was a special time in my progress as a witch when I was becoming accustomed to the power of the Arts and learning that destiny is pre-designed, but open to suggestion, improvement and even alteration. It also taught me that, magick can be like real estate – location, location, location. Last, the opportunity to live in the house as a rental came to me through a series of unlikely events which now seem to me to have been

---

[1] Gaelic term for clockwise movement. In witchcraft movement doesil is used to raise power; to do or to make happen.

arranged. I have believed for a long time that certain houses may choose us as much as we choose them. They "call" to us, some louder than others. I hope you listen.

What kind of witch are you?

The rules of establishing magick space begin with magickal self-awareness. In other words, my magick space is probably not your magick space. The space that I described above worked for me for a myriad of reasons, but every one of them is based on my unique magickal personality. The neutral colors worked for me because, as an artist, color is a blessing, but it can also be a distraction to my ability to concentrate. The smooth stone floor and wall of windows worked for me because I am magickally captivated by surfaces that reflect firelight. To me it is hypnotic and goes straight to the Beta part of my consciuosness. And so on.

If you are as fortunate as I was, you may stumble into your ideal situation. If not, you may have to work for it. Figuring out what things will hinder and what things will help your magickal practice may take some trial and error. Think of it as a puzzle. You may not presently know all the pieces, but you can identify some of them with a little self-analysis.

Let's begin with your outer environment. Are you a desert witch, a sea witch, a mountain witch, or a forest witch? (If you think of yourself as a cyberwitch, this section doesn't really apply.) Many of us have an inexplicable yearning for a particular geographical demonstration of nature's variants. If you're out of sync with your locale and the pull to be elsewhere is very strong, you should listen and take steps to move when you can. If you have longings to be elsewhere, but also have powerfully good reasons to stay where you are, then find a way to compromise.

Here's an example. I'm a forest witch. I live in a semi-tropical forest of pine trees, live oaks, pecans and ash. Most of the houses near me are designed in style and color to blend into the forest, but one house is a mauve, single story, Santa Fe adobe with a tile roof. It is very out of place. I don't know the owners, but I suspect they are out of place as well. However, for whatever reason they find themselves here, they are making the most of it by choosing an immediate environment that is in sync with their geographical preference.

Let your heart speak for your magickal self. Do you love working with one or two of the elements more than others? If so, you can enhance your magickal space with compensations. This is the tricky part. It's very hard to tell whether you will thrive magickally on more or less. For example, if you love working with water, your spells may be more successful if the space is visual water by being blue and audio water by the addition of a fountain, or it could be just the opposite and here's why. You may be drawn to working with water because you're so closely attuned to that element and have so much of it in your personality. In other words, it's easy. Water is home for you; familiar and comfortable. In that case you probably need to compensate balance with significant representations and/or symbols of other elements. The other side of the spectrum is that you may be drawn to working with water because you're magickally thirsty. You need more water in your magickal personality. In that case creating the feeling of living under water could give you and your spellwork a boost. Examples of symbols of water are color, art, reflective surfaces and, of course, the sounds of water. You can also use sea salt to draw your circle and/or anoint yourself with sea water. The possibilities are endless.

Keep in mind that if you are succeeding in your practice you are, by definition, growing and changing. You may need more "water" in your magickal space today, but check in regularly for a shift. When you find that click, that time when all the necessary factors are lined up for your magickal balance, it will feel good, but it will probably be short-lived. Finding the groove means you will grow quickly, magickally speaking, and soon need to make readjustments.

Magickal décor. Less is more.

I would go so far as to suggest that the next time you're making decorating decisions about the place where you will cast spells, you make choices with your magickal eyes. If asked for one rule to follow, I would say that, when it comes to magick space, less is more. Minimal furniture (if any), natural surfaces, natural fabrics, solid colors, neutral colors. This is a good place to begin, a version of stripping away the excess, the unnecessary, the distractions so that you can begin your discovery of what works.

Neatness counts.

At the VERY least, make sure everything within your area of peripheral vision is in order. Your living environment is an extension of you and a reflection of what you think of yourself. At best, actually clean the space – not for dirt. There's nothing dirty about dirt. Clean for dead skin cells, cobwebs and residue left behind in other peoples' fingerprints. Magick space is sacred space. Part of preparation is starting with a clean body and a clean space. You put a little in, you get a little out. You put a lot in, you get a lot out.

As a side note regarding seemingly mundane chores and a desire for better housing (termed "dream homes" in *Seasons*), it's a hard and fast principle of metaphysics and magick as well that you must deserve what you request. If you don't take care of what you have, you won't get very far asking for more. House gods are a particular lot who demand a lot of attention.

A Note on Feng Shui

Feng Shui is based on the idea that there is magick in the placement of things. While this is true, the practical application of Feng Shui is problematic for a lot of reasons. The first and biggest problem is that the magick of Feng Shui is intertwined with Asian culture to the point where it is almost inextricable. And cultural influence just can't be arbitrarily proclaimed irrelevant. That influence is too much a part of who we are. A couple or three small examples. 1.) Before we even start school we, as Westerners, already have an understanding on some level that green and gold represent prosperity in our culture. If you were in China, the same would be true of the color red. 2.) In Asia, beamed ceilings are thought to be architecturally disastrous to good fortune. But the English built an empire during a time when most buildings had beamed ceilings. 3.) Last, there's little that will make you feel sillier than a Buddhist chant, if you're not indoctrinated Buddhist.

While my criticisms and examples could go on for quite awhile, I still think there is something to this. Couldn't agree more, for instance, about the inherent magick present in mirrors. (See *The Shadow Magicks of Reflective Surfaces* in Chapter 13.) Part of Feng Shui is common sense; things such as getting rid of clutter because organized thought cannot thrive in an environement of chaos and arranging your work space so as to be aware when others are approaching.

If you have not been exposed and are interested, I suggest Terah Kathryn Collins' series beginning with *The Western Guide to Feng Shui*.

Smells

As a group witches tend to like animals and usually live with one or more. Animals are marvelous gifts, but they do come with extra house-keeping chores.

Avoid synthetic perfumes and artificial scents if you can for a lot of reasons, some magickal, some mundane. From a mundane standpoint, lots of people have bad reactions to synthetic candles that appear in the form of headaches, but they don't put the two things together. You may not be one of these, but you might have a guest who is. When I wear a scent deliberately I use one or a combination of essential oils (real) that are safe to apply directly to skin. They last, have impact, will not become foul and stale on your clothing and engage your magickal mind. If you burn candles, I strongly recommend unscented. Essential oils cannot be folded into wax. Candles advertised as "essential oil candles" just have a superficial coating that will immediately burn off when it contacts flame. If you want to anoint a candle with an essential oil for magickal purposes, start with an unscented candle and do it yourself.

Home Security

I know a woman who says she prefers smaller residences because she doesn't want to have to psychically protect a large place awake and asleep. That is, most likely, a valid method for property protection, but it would be better to conserve that energy for other usage if you can. See Barrier Spells for Protection in Chapter 12.

Familiars

I do agree with Feng Shui that animals add life and energy to our space. Pets, on the physical plane, can be famliars, but pets are not always familiars just because they belong to witches. In fact, it's rather unusual. I have had animals all my life. All were worth having, but none of them has been a familiar. I did have occasion to see one though.

A few years ago a friend was beset by a campaign of psychic attack in the form of dream invasion. The violator was an ex-husband. Her health and sense of well-being were going downhill. So I agreed to perform a banishing for the friend whose sister was also going to be present and assist. I went to her apartment on a rainy night. I had a cup of tea while drying off and said hello to the cat lying on the bed, who was thoroughly unimpressed the way only cats can be.

My friend, who was the victim, had never cast in her home before. We moved some living room furniture to make room. I told the others what to expect, performed a protection on the premises to keep the ne'er-do-well's spirit outside. Then I cast a circle. The cat came trotting in look-ing very interested and ran right to the invisible edge of our circle. We watched in amazement as she began to walk doesil around the edge of our unseen circle. She would take one step and then paw the air as if she was trying to locate a boundary. When she seemed satisfied that she knew where it was, she would take another couple of steps. We were much too fascinated to interrupt the dance. She continued in this fashion for a few minutes until she found a place that satisfied her mysterious goal. There she sat looking intently at the circle before her, ears pointed forward, tail moving back and forth behind her as if she had a fix on prey. The purring was so loud we had to smile ourselves.

We determined that we would proceed as four rather than three. When the spell was complete, I closed the circle and felt good about the results. The cat got up, walked straight across the area where the circle had been, left the room, restaked her claim on the bed and resumed looking every bit as uninterested as before.

No indeed. Familiars are not just witch's pets.

SECTION II WHAT YOU NEED

Chapter 9 Tools

Tools in order of importance

1.)   You are the only tool you can't do without. If you were stranded on an island with nothing, you could still perform magick and do it well.

2.)   So far as external tools, I think *Seasons of the Witch* is the most valuable, but I could be biased. This is because identification of the perfect time to cast is crucial. *Seasons* can do multi-layered duty as book of days, [1]Book of Shadows and Light, and journal. This is particularly true of the binder version of the Daily to which you can add pages at will.

3.)   Your surroundings can be a hindrance to magick which demands compensatory measures *(see Magick Space)* or the site where you will cast can create a magickal atmosphere that is itself a tool.

[1]**Books of Shadows and Light** -A Book of Shadows reflects the path of the owner and develops a theme that compliments the witch's focus. That may be recipes, healing remedies, records of the personal journey, goals and aspirations, rituals, spells and even dreams. Sometimes books that concentrate on spells also record the results of spellcasting much the same as the careful notations of scientific experiment.

Some of the traditions that have been attached to these texts include burning the book upon the death of the owner and taboos on selling any of the information for money.

Like most things pagan, there is disagreement about the details of Books of Shadows. One of the first controversies concerns what to call it. Is it a Book of Shadows or a grimoire, neither or both? Many witches draw no distinction between the two. Others say the Book of Shadows contains rites and the history of events while a grimoire concentrates on spells, symbols, potions, etc. Covens usually maintain a group Book Shadows, but the individuals within the coven keep their own personal book as well. Some witches share their B.O.S. information openly. Others insist that a B.O.S. loses both its value and power if its secrecy is compromised. (See *Book of Shadows Esbat Blessing*, Chap. 12.)

4.)   A compass or knowledge of direction in reference to your circle. Whether the placement of the Earth pillar is north or east according to the system you're using, you must know where north and east are.

5.)   A focus. Your circle should have a central focus. It could be a cauldron (or facsimile), a candle, a pentagram, a tarot spread, a letter, etc. It could be just about anything that graphically characterizes the purpose of the spell. The main thing is to center the object of focus in your circle so that it becomes the cog of the wheel of your spell. Tarot cards are excellent for this purpose. *See Intro Section III.*

6.)   Salt. I don't know why salt is so magickal. I just know that it is. I use rock salt in magick because it comes with two blessings. First, it's earth with magickal properties and, second, it looks like small crystals so it's pretty, too. If I'm doing a spell that is important and/or serious in nature, I use rock salt to draw my circle into an absolute seal after I'm inside. It forms a barrier that can't be crossed without my specific invitation or permission. That, in turn, frees me to concentrate my attention elsewhere. (Added bonus: It's easy to sweep up afterward.)

If I need to perform some magickal feat on the spur of the moment and don't have time for a formal, bathing ritual, I go to the kitchen sink, get my face, hands, arms and chest wet and rub ordinary cooking salt over the moist skin. It instantly transforms one into majician extraordinaire. (This isn't practical if you wear much make-up or if you have any open cuts or scratches on your skin, but I suspect it doubles as a nice, natural exfoliant.)

7.)   Something precious from your childhood that serves as a reminder that you are unique and native to this dimension.

8.)   Everything else.

Tools don't have to come from a store with a label that says "magickal tool". They don't necessarily have to come with a price tag either. If you're walking in a dry river bed and you feel compelled to pick up a rock, it could be useful to you magickally. Everything you see around you is a potential magick tool; objects and events like a moonrise.

Drama (High Magick)

Paraphernalia doesn't equal magick, but it certainly can set a mood and remind you where you are and what you're doing. If I need to make an impression on my magickal mind, I mount a production. I suspect that there's a little drama in every witch. Encourage the magickal child in you to come out and play. Encourage the wizard in you to make an appearance.

The thing about elaborate magicks, especially the kind that take a lot out of you physically, is that the next time you need to address the same issue, the amount of energy required will be less. Repeated visits will eventually produce a sort of automation. At some point your magickal mind will proceed without deliberate engagement and instruction from your conscious mind; much like learning to drive a car. Watch out for the pitfalls of the sorceror's apprentice. If, at any point, you suspect your magickal mind may have misunderstood a direction, take steps to correct before somebody gets hurt. (See *Reversals.*)

A few don'ts.

1.) Don't buy or use a tool because other people do.

2.) Don't employ the same tools every time you cast a spell. You need to use your tools in different ways for different spells for the same reason you would choose different positions in love-making. Monotony will give your magick the doldrums and magickal forces will not cooperate if excitement is absent from the process.

3.) Don't wear red to a casting unless you're very experienced, able to recognize when unseen entities are present, able to distinguish their intent and able to control the proceedings. The thing about red is that it attracts lots of interest and curiosity, good and bad.

Witchy Trivia. Plants and ingredients for magick and healing used to be given code names such as Eye of Newt and Bats Wing.

Something Wiccan This Way Comes

Double, double toil and trouble
Fire burn and cauldron bubble
Watch the pot for simmer and shake
Scale of dragon, tooth of snake

In the Grimoire there by spells
of wand and knife and ne'er-do-well's.
Root of hemlock dug in dark
in the fire a merry spark.

Huddle round the flames now sing
Elementals in a ring.
Feather, herb and graveyard dirt
You can do if none be hurt.

Whirl and twirl and learn The Rede
Rule of Three and mind the Hede
by flying besoms, Harvest Moon,
witches' letters rune by rune.

Fay familiars spread the tale
o'er forest, stream and hill and dale
and cause the pricking of our thumbs
when something Wiccan this way comes.

- Danann 2002

SECTION III

PowerCasting™ *Seasons of the Witch*

First, what is PowerCasting™?

PowerCasting™ is my system for identifying power days for spell casting purposes. This is the most efficient way to find optimum times for working in cooperation with natural law. I call these "power" days simply because the magickal power available to you is increased during certain hours - sometimes a little, sometimes a lot. Lesser energies are identified by lower case letters. Major energies are capitalized. Extremely powerful energy, usually occurring just a few times a year, is capitalized, in bold letters and, if it's magickal in nature, will have an exclamation point as well.

These identifiers refer to potential objects of spellwork.

Sometimes the object is an essence.
Sometimes it is a thing.

Sometimes the energy is right for pulling to you; attraction, magnetizing or manifesting.

Sometimes the energy calls for pushing away; banishing, repelling or reversing.

You will find that use of this system saves you many hours, days really, each year of research that would be typical for a committed practice of the Craft.

Seasons has been designed to meld the magickal with the mundane partly because of the organization requirements of modern life and the pace of modern life, but there's more to it than that. The fact that your next sales appointment or doctor appointment or reminder to pick up dry cleaning is on the same page with a spellcasting opportunity or pagan holy day is a constant reminder to you that you are more than the pay you earn and the errands you run. Even if you used *Seasons of the Witch* once or twice a year for spellcasting purposes, it still serves its purpose as that bridge to your magickal life.

Spellwork

The vast majority of people in the world never make changes until there is a crisis sufficient enough to spur them into action. Even the threat of life or death is often not compelling enough. Environmental issues are an example of this. (I fear that, by the time enough people are motivated to a state of concern, it will be far too late to save the beautiful planet's ability to sustain animal life, but I digress.)

Spellwork is a highbrow activity in that people who are so engaged are showing up for their lives. They are present when roll is called and are actively participating. Further, they demonstrate an impressive level of development by pursuing a result, and therefore gratification, that will almost certainly be delayed.[1]

I salute all of you. However ironic, and amusing, it may be, you are leaders among your race.

Quick Spells

This is not a compromise of my strong position on writing your own spells. Everyone draws inspiration from some influence or other. "Quick Spells" are suggestions for tools you might incorporate into a spell that is on the lightweight end of importance. Being indicted for a felony would be a matter of heavyweight importance. Getting your errands run with time to catch up on previously recorded soaps is of lightweight importance

8 day rituals

Sometimes major power energy for a spell focus will emerge on a given day two weeks in a row such as two Sundays in a row or two Tuesdays

[1]There is a strong correlation between the length of time an organism is willing to wait for gratification and its place on the philogenetic scale. The longer the wait, the more developed the organism is considered to be. It seems reasonable that this proposition would also apply to individuals with a species. Brain surgeons, for example, are practically middle-aged before they even begin their careers. The first half of their lives is spent in training for the rest.

in a row. This occurrence presents an opportunity for an eight day spell which I term "ritual" to connote a methodical approach to a matter of greater importance. An eight day ritual should be planned as a single expenditure of energy spread over a period of eight days. Usually some action is taken each day to renew the commitment of energy.

Color Notations with Power Days

Colors are mentioned only when they make a *significant* difference. The selection of colors is normally considered part of writing your spell or ritual. For help with this process, see the chart of *Light and Shadow Aspects of Color* in Chapter 12.

The Days of the Week

The days of the week are listed in their original form as a reminder that we, as a people, are pagan in our roots.

the Tarot Planner part of Seasons

As many of you already know, the tarot is used most often for divination. We are great proponents of the divining powers of tarot, but tarot references in *Seasons* pertain to adaptation of tarot as a tool for spellwork.

It is impossible to define tarot in a paragraph, but here are the most rudimentary basics. There are 78 cards in most decks. The Major Arcana consists of 22 cards representing archetypes[1] of life passages and experience.The Minor Arcana consists of 56 cards divided into 4 suits of 14 each. There are 10 numbered cards (Ace through 10) and 4 court cards (King, Queen, Knight, Page). Each suit symbolizes an ancient element. Cups (Water), Pentacles (Earth), Swords (Air), Wands (Fire). Each card represents an influence in our lives and experience.

Individual tarot cards create an instant point of focus that captures the attention of your magickal mind with qualifications. You must use a card that compliments the essence of that which you wish to accomplish with

[1]Archetype is the way Jung explained universal psychological patterns.

your spell AND you must use a deck that is magick as art (and not just art). If these conditions are met, then even if you are not a student of tarot and not acquainted with its subtleties, your magickal mind will recognize the symbols and respond.

There are hundreds of decks available. Some of them are collectible as art. Some are capricious. Some are comical or even silly. Only a few are designed for use as magickal tools. There is a good reason why the baseline standard for beginning tarot studies is Rider Waite. It is an excellent example of a deck with archetypal symbolism that can't be beat even if the art is less appealing than others. We can also recommend Hanson Roberts and the Druid Craft Tarot which is available at www.7th-House. com because it's difficult to find in the U.S. You will also find illustrations herein from a couple of other decks. The Golden Tarot has appealing imagery and is usually on the mark magickally.

Also read *Magick and Tarot* by Kelly Danann, 2007, published by 7th House.

Note on choosing a deck for divination purposes. Consistency is less important when you're choosing a deck for spellwork because you're normally working with one or two cards at a time. In divination, however, it's important that all the cards maintain the look and feel of the deck as a whole. It sounds simple, but you'd be surprised how few decks meet this standard. Turning up a card that doesn't seem to belong when you're in a magickal zone is as disconcerting as having an actor break the "fourth wall" and speak directly to the audience in the middle of a play. Before you buy a deck for divination purposes, make sure you've seen *all* the cards.

Quatrains

The quatrain is an integral part of basic spellwork and one of the most essential building blocks of our witchcraft heritage. It is a four line rhyme form of poetry ideally suited for chants and incantations. The quality of the poetry is irrelevant as the point is to make an impression on the magickal mind or to attract the attention of elementals, deities or other helpers whom you might wish to summon.

When written for the purpose of casting a spell, they are charms to be chanted. They appeal directly to the subconscious mind especially when repeated again and again, minimum three times. It's impossible to say how many times you should repeat your charm because the number is unique to the task and the witch. The best advice I can give is to memorize your quatrain and begin repeating it slowly while you are engaged in activities such as preparing for your spell. Continue saying it until it feels "done" (fully cooked).

When I am so engaged, I have found that, chants begins to take on a cadence of their own as if using my voice as a tool. At some point the repetitions get faster, faster, faster then abruptly end.

never say never because it's a negative

Above all, please remember NOT to use negatives such as NOT in your quatrain. The subconscious mind doesn't hear these English language stepchildren, but ignores them and proceeds as if the statement were a positive. For instance, if you say, "The postman will not bite the dog on the next full moon" your magickal mind will hear, "The postman *will* bite the dog on the next full moon." Avoid all negative modifiers in your chants and spell directives.

Here are some examples of quatrains for the purpose of conveying form. Use for inspiration, but remember that quatrains of your own authorship are most powerful.

Book of Shadows, Book of Light
bide with me this dark moon night.
Magicks, charms and witches' dreams
All are sacred. Blessed be.

Bend me, shape me, make me fluid.
As accomplished as a Druid.
Inner secret, shadow thin
In be out and out be in.

By light of sun, the charm's begun
By dark of night the spell is right
Goddess guide my way this hour
lend your daughter witch's power

Each candle I burn tonight
releases bad that causes blight.
Bid me walk the path of light
Feelings now calm to quiet.

Chapter 10 The Moons.
Wax on. Wax off.

Our Source
Our astrological reference is the *Ephemerides*, The Rosicrucian Ephemeris 2000-2100, international edition.

Lunar Astrology

We begin with the proposition that the moon rules magick on Earth. *Seasons* PowerCasting™ system is based on lunar astrology meaning that the movements of the moon in relationship to the Earth and its monthly passage through the twelve signs of the zodiac (see also are crucial to a successful practice. Magickal workings, spells and rituals planned in cooperation with the moon and stars could be compared to rowing downstream. While some effort may still be required, it is faster, easier and, most important, possible.

Most people appreciate the sight of a full moon. It's representation in art and literature express its place of importance in human experience, but witches seem to have an even greater appreciation, one that could almost be called a bond. Although it doesn't happen often, I have been awakened by the full moon in the middle of the night and "beckoned", if you will, to get out of bed and follow the trail of light to a window for no reason other than to admire a particularly magickal song.

Calendars Magickal and Mundane

The present twelve-month calendar, known as Gregorian, was devised by Roman Catholics and was not accepted by Britain and its colonies (that means us) until 1752. In 2006 I first introduced an alterate witches' calendar based on thirteen moon cycles in a year. The moon's gravitational pull controls the tides, is responsible for collective human mood swings and should be taken into account when deciding times of planting and harvest as has been done for generations (i.e., *Poor Richards Almanac*). The number of moons in a year is also the same as the number of menses cycles and, probably, biocycles in general regardless of sex or age. To me a calendar based on the moon is more than good magickal sense. To me it would seem to be good sense in general. So I devised a calendar of based on the moons of a given year. These dates were published side by side with the Gregorian calendar with the intention of creating a magickal alternative. The names of the thirteen months of my Witches' Lunar Calendar and their meanings, are published in Chapter 12.

Esbats

Simply put, esbats are full moons. They are times of heightened magickal energy traditionally used for gatherings and the collective workings of covens, but also ideal for work as a solitary. The first page of *Seasons* always lists the year's Esbats under the Wheel of the Year, the dates when they will occur and their specific names. These are not names taken from one of the traditions of moon-naming. These are names that have been given to a particular Esbat according to the energy of that particular moon.

Many of the names given to Esbats in *Seasons* are unique to that particular moon. Others may recur from time to time. To me this is many times for magickal and valuable than the rote acquisition of a system that applied to another place in another time. Because the names of Esbats are dependent upon the moon's particular energy when it passes through a house of the zodiac, on rare occasions the East Coast and West Coast may celebrate with different Esbat names during the same month.

Moons were originally given names by various traditions to convey something magickally or mystically relevant to the people of that time and place. If "Corn Moon" doesn't engage you emotionally, it will not have any magickal *meaning* for you. That is what we are attempting to recreate here.

Wishing Moons

Wishing moons occur four times a year on the full moon closest to the sabbats. They are occasions for planning the goals of the coming quarter and assessing the results of the quarter past.

Moon Void of Course

The moon completes a revolution around the Earth every 29 days, passing through the 12 signs of the zodiac and spending about 2 1/2 days in each sign. The delay that occurs between leaving one house of the zodiac and entering another is called Moon Void Of Course. It is a time during which the moon is not ruled or influenced by any sign. (Technically put, the moon is void of course during the time between making its last major aspect to a planet in one sign and its entry into the next sign.) It can last from a few seconds (rare) to more than two days.

Spellwork must only be performed when the moon is present in one of the houses of the zodiac. When the moon is in transition spell results will be nullified at best and reverse or go awry at worst. This is why there are time and sign notations on every applicable day of the year. They are delineated into the four time zones of the Continental U.S. not because we think you don't know how to subtract an hour or three going west, but because days of the week also play a part in determining prime energy for spellwork. If the moon is in house transit when the day changes, the spellwork opportunities can be very different depending upon time zone. It's a big continent.

A *Seasons* notation of "NO SPELLS" simply means the moon is void of course for the entire day. This happens two or three times a year.

In summary, *do not cast when the moon is void of course.*

Mercury Retrograde

We include notations when Mercury is retrograde mainly because many *Seasons* users keep track. Basically Mercury Retrograde means that three times each year, for about twenty-two days, the planet Mercury appears to move backward through the zodiac from the perspective of Earth. Many people swear that things electric become temperamental during Mercury Retrograde. Others see this period more literally in the sense of the god, Mercury, messenger to the gods, moving backwards and believe the period interferes with efficient errand running.

Waxing and Waning

The period between the new moon and the full moon is waxing energy which is ideal for spells to draw things to you; things being essences, activities, opportunities or material goods. This is the area shaded yellow on *Seasons on the Wall* and on the month-at-a-glance sections of *Seasons Weekly* and *Seasons Daily* planners. The rest of the month is waning energy suitable for tearing down what's not working for you, reversing mistakes or wrong directions, generally pushing the unwanted away. People often make the mistake of concentrating on waxing phases and ignoring the rest until a crisis gets their attention. That behavior is both beneath you and not in your best interest. If you want to get the biggest bang from your practice of magick, use the push as well as the pull. Consider the following.

One of the facts of physics that we as witches or majicians work with is vacuum effect. The two properties of vacuums that concern magick are first, that a vacuum must be created in order to add something new to a finite area of containment, in this case the area of containment is you rendered finite by your spirit's occupation of a physical body. And, second, that a vacuum, once created, will seek to be filled. This applies to the material and the nonmaterial. The point in regard to your magickal work is this.

When you realize that you require an adjustment in some area, making space for that new thing makes the manifestation easier and quicker. For example, let's say you want to attract the love of your life. You plan and begin a serious, magickal campaign toward the realization of this goal. Meanwhile, you are living with a good-for-nothing boyfriend who is the antithesis of making your dreams come true. If your magickal work is successful, your magick will locate the person who is also hoping for you and start them on their journey in your direction (or v.v.). If you are available emotionally and physically, you've created a vacuum with room for this love of your life to fill. If not, you are requiring your spells do double duty.because, in order to fulfill your goal, your magick must find this person, bring them to you PLUS get rid of the good-for-nothing-boyfriend. It can be done, but it will take more time and take more out of you.

All magick is Chaos Magick

All magick is Chaos Magick. Magick imposes upon the status quo and demands that things be rearranged to match the expectations or demands of the majician.

Yes. Creating vacuums does cause temporary chaos, but good things come from chaos; not just the arrival of the new thing you want, but also the excitement of transition and knowing that you're an active participant in your own life; that is as opposed to being like a mindless leaf floating on a fast-moving river doomed to always be caught off guard by what happens next.

Chapter 11 Power Opportunities

Magickal Notation on NonSpell Activity

For the most part the purpose of magickal notation in *Seasons* is to identify periods when spells with a particular goal may be cast with results compounded and/or improved due to the cooperative nature of the energy at that particular time and day. However, a few items with day and time notation are instructions to act in the moment rather than to cast into the future. Following is that list. If an item does not appear on this list, it means the mention is an indication that the energy should be channeled into a spell for that thing or essence.

Art Projects - Physical action and/or spellwork. For detailed explanation see this designation under alphabetical list of Power Days.

Divination -   Decide what you want to know and ask using your favorite tool(s) for that purpose.

Gatherings -   A good time to meet and share with magickal friends or associates formally or otherwise.

Honor ancestors - In any way you see fit.

Initiations -   Of any kind.

Networking -   This means actual networking as in physically going to a breakfast for that purpose, scheduling lunches, making phone calls, etc.

Planning -   Self-explanatory.

Planting -   Applies to the actual physical planting in the earth or to the symbolic planting of seeds for growth of a business or dream home or whatever project has your fascination.

Psychic Development - Take deliberate steps to improve your intuition, astral travel, reading of cards, scrying, etc.

Reflection / Self-Assessment - You cannot chart your course without an accurate read on where you are. This is a time to ask yourself questions such as, How am I doing? Am I on the right path? What do I really want? Is there something more I could do to get what I want? Work with the Element of Water.

Work in the Astral - Astral work is an advanced magickal activity. The mention of the opportunity is not intended as an enticement, but rather as an announcement to those who are trained or naturally inclined. Watch for notes warning against working with electricity. This means using something electrical in or nearby your circle.

Work in Book of Shadows - The process of actually sitting in front of your book and giving it some attention. Use the time for whatever the book needs whether that is organization, spell creativity, the journaling of thoughts with magickal bent or origins, etc. Your book becomes more precious, valuable and life-like with use.

Work with Familiars - All pets are not familiars, as you know, but all pets need attention. If you do have a familiar, design a spell that requires their participation and schedule it for a Work with Familiars power day.

Written communication - If it needs to be said in writing, this would be a good time. THIS DOES NOT MEAN E-MAIL!! If it's important and social in nature, do it the old-fashioned way. Get beautiful, heavy paper that's wonderful to touch and write your message in your own hand as if it was a work of art. If it must be magick, seal it with your intention and wax as well.

Most of the Power Day terms listed in this section occur every year, many of them on multiple occasions within a year, but some occur only rarely. There are, I'm certain, some energies that may arise in future years and, therefore, cannot appear on this list as the whole of the thing is based on linear time. Also, many of the terms are different from others in subtle ways, but I expect that those who gravitate toward witchcraft are capable of discriminating between fine layers of distinction.

These have been divided into two lists, one waxing, one waning.

Waxing	Notes
adventure	More excitment, heightened feeling of "aliveness". This is an "A" ticket ride. The caveat here is that adventure isn't always comfortable. I rarely travel with groups, but was with one in Florence many years ago. My companion and I were separated from the rest and spent some time running through the labyrinthe of the oldest part of the city thinking we were lost. On telling this to the tour guide later he laughed and said, "There are worse things than being lost in Florence." The remark turned out to be a profundity I have recalled countless times. The point of

The point of view expresses words to live by. The experience was unsettling at the time, but I wouldn't take anything for it.

Adventure is often paired with opportunity as there is so much adventure in opportunity and so much opportunity in adventure.

Most people tiptoe through life hoping to make it safely to death.
   - Bob Proctor

Tarot card: The Fool. Color: Red

Waxing	Notes
ambition	Figure out what you need before you ask for it. It's usually better to address the cause than the effect. If you think you don't have enough energy to follow through on getting what you want, it may not be energy you need more of. It may be ambition. It's the original energizer. Why, one might ask, would anyone be interested in casting a spell to stimulate ambition? Ambition is the beginning of a logical progression toward success. Sometimes we find ourselves in conflict over our need to be complacent and our need to achieve, attain or conquer. If procrastination, laziness or lack of energy gets in the way of your dreams and goals, you might consider a plan that includes spellwork for prodding your ambitious self into life.
	If the main ingredient you lack is energy or enough enthusiasm to see your goal through to success, the Ace of Wands (Rods, Staves, Clubs) is a good choice for a one card spell. Ambition is a member of the fire family, a child of ego and the sex drive. It is always depicted as vertical, erect if you will, and usually glowing with pride and promise. Its essence is masculine, active and pronounced. Its presence is accompanied by a feeling of "aliveness".
art projects	In ancient Greece every soldier was expected to pursue a gentle art to balance the martial art. You don't have to wait until you "retire". You don't need to share your art with anyone else if you don't want to, but you must find a creative outlet because we all need it for health of body and spirit.
	Recommended reading: Julia Cameron *The Artist's Way*.
	If you happen to work in a field that is art related or uses art in some way, don't miss these opportunities as inspiration is available for brilliance. Also, the term could also be read as "projects" in the arts as the energy applies to

Waxing	Notes
art projects (cont'd.)	writing and music as well as applied arts such as painting and sculpting. *Use for physical action or for "spells to call a Muse".* Tarot Card: The Eight of Pentacles represents the practice necessary for mastery of a skill. When this card appears in a spread it means that preparation will meet opportunity for material gain or personal satisfaction. When used to enhance a spell working, it represents speeding up the preparation process or enhancing the end result. Color: Purple, gods: The Muses
attraction	Attraction is a simple word with complicated levels. You can use this energy to strengthen your power to magnetize things or people in the sense of social desirability whether your goal is political viability or seduction. Tarot Card: Ace of Cups, Color - appropriate to object.
balance	We live in a time where excess is often admired and rewarded. Ex. Although "workaholism" might render creature comforts or status, the ultimate price (there's always a price), is health and, often, happiness. If circumstances block balance, correct here. Tarot Card: The Chariot represents the experience of being pulled in different, sometimes opposite, directions. Yet more control over conflicting interests and responsibilities is possible, especially with magickal support as beautifully illustrated by this particular image. Color: Brown
barrier spells for security	Tarot Card: The World. Call on the four corners, always present, always surrounding you, to protect you from unwanted energies, entities or people. I use lower level, earth elementals as guards around the perimeter of my property; ideally suited to the task because they are not smart enough to think for themselves, but more than strong enough to meet any challenge. PLUS they're happy to do it as it makes them feel important and useful. I learned a valuable lesson regarding this practice which

Waxing	Notes
barrier spells for security (cont'd.)	I want to pass on to you.
	Years ago when I was renting a house, the one mentioned in "Ideal Space" in Chapter 8. The entire neighborhood was being reconceived because the land was valuable. The old homes were torn down so that the estate-sized lots could accommodate new, faux chateaus clustered so close together they almost shared walls. My landlord wanted to sell his property and retire on the profit. It broke my heart when he did not renew my lease, but life is change.
	A little over a year later I drove by the old address to see what had happened to my magick house. The entire neighborhood had been covered in new monstrosities except for the land where I had lived. It was still for sale. I must have groaned out loud because I knew instantly that I had moved away, but left the sentries at their post. They, being dumb but loyal and committed, would have stayed there until the end of time.
	I still feel horrible about the incident to this day. I did a terrible disservice to my former landlord and to my guards who behaved so admirably even for so unworthy a majician as myself. I begged their forgiveness and dismissed them. After some time had passed, they were happily reassigned. As for the property, once the invisible barriers were cleared, it changed hands right away.
	The moral of the story should be evident. If you cast a barrier spell to secure something you own, don't forget to reverse it when a change is made. OR, perhaps better, you can build in a fail safe release such as "until I move away or pass away whichever shall occur sooner". This is one of the few magicks I know that does not seem to demonstrate entropy.

Waxing	Notes
beauty	See Health / Healing.
Beginnings, Changes	These two are always paired because they're Siamese twins. Tarot Card: The Wheel of Fortune is a visual reminder of such adages as "the only constant is change" and "all things must pass". You can either proactively participate in the shaping of things to come or wait to be victimized by random chance. One of magick's highest and best uses is in assisting the practitioner with channeling this inevitable change in a desired direction. Color: Red
Borrow or Lend Money	Not to be read as a recommendation for either but, if this is your intention, you can smooth the way for borrowing with a spell using the Queen of Pentacles. You can also use the same focus to protect the return of your funds with interest. Do not allow the Queen's generous side to gain control of your lending impulses. Colors: Green for borrowing, Black for lending.
business	(new) Tarot Card: Ace of Pentacles, Color: Green
business plans	This applies to new business as well as to expansion or improvement. The Emperor is one of three cards that could be put to use here, the others being the Two of Wands (Rods or Staves) or the King of Pentacles (Coins) The Emperor symbolizes worldly success. He is archetype of mastery of creative ideas that manifest in worldly abundance He brings focus, decisiveness and authority to your project. Color: Green IV L'Empereur IV L'Imperatore *IV The Emperor* IV Der Herrscher IV El Emperador Hanson-Roberts Tarot

Waxing	Notes
career	Your magickal success relies upon a support system of common sense and education. Casting won't help you unless you've already made adequate preparation in the mundane sphere. After you have acquired the credentials and experience necessary for the position or situation you seek, along with a practical education regarding how a successful person in your field would dress, speak, stand, sit, behave, etc., you may expect career spells to manifest opportunities. Career Spells The Page of Pentacles Candle Color: Green
clarity for decisions	Use for dilemmas. Tarot Card: The Sun is an excellent card for spells to help see things more clearly. Because sub-themes of clairvoyance are present we recommend the color: Lilac. or White
clubs	see Networking in nonSpell activity.
collect debts or favors	Here is one of my exceptions to the rule against compelling another person to action. It may even be a company or institution that has a debt outstanding to you. Giving someone who owes you money a nudge in the direction of doing what's right could only be good for both of you. You get your money. They get the debt off their conscience or their books. Tarot card: Six of Pentacles. Three states of being are portrayed. Focus on the aspect that applies to your situation. Are you the giver, the receiver or the needy?
communication	Also often paired with negotiation. From a certain point of view, most communication is also negotiation.
contracts	A good time to cast a spell over a contract to be negotiated, drawn or signed so that all is at least fair and at best in your favor. Color: Dark Blue, God: Thoth
courage	Often paired with warrior energy. Both are born from a need for success or victory in some area. If you need courage for the accomplishment of a feat, do the work magickally first. Tarot Card: The Six of Wands, Rods or Staves. Color: Red, Goddess: Diana

Waxing	Notes
creativity	Face it. All animals eat, work, play and procreate. The spark that makes us aspire to be gods is creativity. Witchcraft is not so simple as following the directions of recipes. You must bring imagination to your practice along with a willingness to fail. Tarot Card: The Page of Wands can be used for spells to facilitate work with crafts, to gain inspiration for art or to promote the development of talent. Among other things, this card symbolizes untapped potential. Color: Creativity in Magick - Deep Purple, Art - Purple, Talent - White, Crafts - Orange, Home Crafts - Yellow, gods: The Muses
divination	Invoke the goddess Theia. Don't overlook opportunities to sharpen your skill. If you don't already have a divining tool of choice, experiment until you find one that feels like a magickal partner. Use your power opportunities for Divination well by having a list of questions. This is a tradition inherited from gypsies. So far as I know, no group is better. However, when it comes to sharing what they see, they don't pull any punches and, to me, this becomes an ethical question regarding harm. I knew a woman whose job it was to hire fortune tellers for a local Renaissance Faire. She told me that she had hired a gypsy the year before who was very good except that she had no sense of what not to reveal. A young couple expecting their first baby came in for a reading. The reader proceeded to tell them, in the bloodiest terms, about a pending childbirth disaster. The ethical question is this. If you don't relate what you "see" then you're not being truthful. That might be a compromise of integrity. If telling what you see could do harm, as in this case where worry could be bad for both mother or baby, then I have to go with compromising integrity. This should be high up in Witches' Ethics.

Waxing	Notes
domestic power	Everybody should get their way sometimes. Balance is key. If you are a woman in a shared-environment relationship with a man who is not wiccae, at times you will undoubtedly find yourself in a struggle for equal say. Spellwork is less wear and tear on everyone than fighting it out toe-to-toe. If you are paired with someone whose true heart requires dominance of others, you may have little success. However, if your mate is of good character, but merely misguided or uneducated, persistent casting will, over time, reap the mutually satisfying rewards of domestic partnership.

Tarot: Look to the Queens for help.

The Queen of Cups. Triumph through acquiescence. Color: Brown

The Queen of Swords. Persuasion through logic and debate. Color: Dark Blue

The Queen of Pentacles. Resolving a monetary disagreement in your favor. Color: Dark Green or Gold

The Queen of Wands. Triumph by seduction or magick.

Queen of Cups

Waxing	Notes
dream homes	If you are conjuring a dream home, don't forget to add magickal necessities and desires to the list. See Magick Space, Chapter 8. Tarot Card: Ten of Cups, Color: Brown
earthy passions	For millenia certain religious persuasions have done their best to convince people that we should not be "in the world"; that we should turn away from earth's pleasures in favor of concentrating on the hereafter. Pagans are rarely the ethereal sort (and some know how to feast like Vikings) so this probably doesn't apply to you. However, if you suspect that, in comparison to others.... ...you're not enjoying the sunset as much ...you don't find the comical as funny ...you don't like Mexican food ...you don't think sex is all it's cracked up to be ...you may not be getting as much out of the experience of being in a body as you could. Call on Pan.

Waxing	Notes
education	The process of learning usually means replacing previously held beliefs, opinions or thoughts with new ones which, although productive on many levels, creates mental chaos or upheaval. We cannot escape the fact that human nature predisposes us to complacence. That makes almost any desired change a challenge; a conflict between acting in our own future best interest and our desire to settle into a "comfort zone". Tarot Card: The Knight of Swords. The suit of air, or intellect, governs traditional learning. This is the card of mind expansion and new perspectives. The Knight is brilliant and also fearless in his pursuit of new knowledge. Colors: Dark Blue for intellectual support, Orange for resolve to untertake the unknown Note: If the issue is funding an education, use one of the spells for money. See also Higher Learning Magickal Arts. Illustration from Tarot of Prague.

Waxing	Notes
elemental magick	Elemental magick, in this reference, refers to elements expressed as manifest entities. Elementals are amenable to helping those who help themselves. If you expect a free ride and have no intention of doing your part, they will ignore you at best and punish you for asking at worst. For example, don't bother to ask gnomes for help with money matters if you haven't taken serious steps toward sound money management practices.

Elementals can travel freely between dimensions, but don't usually make themselves known unless they have a good reason to do so. Also, Elemental Magick *in the Astral*.

An opportunity to perform elemental magick in the astral is for adepts with great confidence and skill. If you're not there yet, please stay home!

This image from *The Gothic Tarot* by Joseph Vargo could have been designed as an illustration for Elemental Magick in the Astral.

Waxing	Notes
fair deals	Fair Deals power days are cousins to Justice. A Fair Deals spell would be appropriate when you have good reason to believe you won't receive fair treatment in a given situation without magickal intervention. Tarot Card: Judgment
feminine, maternal, domestic issues	Hearth energy to be used to improve things close to home, for health issues of a feminine nature and any domestic issue that needs redress. Tarot Card: The Empress represents feminine fertility, the ability to create abundance in environment along with familial content and new life. This card can also be used for spells to promote domestic harmony.
financial gain	To be used when you're doing pretty well, but want to do better. Not for people who overspend or have significant financial liabilities. You must master managing what you have before the powers of the earth will find you worthy to receive more. Tarot Card: The Three of Pentacles (or "Coins") is the card of readiness. The structure of the desired goal is in place in the realm of imagination. Preparation is complete. Results are on the way, but need a final boost of energy, hard work or magick to manifest in the material world. Color: Green
fire energy	Use for any issue that would require passion or intensity.
friendship	Friendship spells are distinct from popularity spells and social success spells because the focus here is on an *authentic* connection with another person who will honor the relationship as you would. Tarot Card: The Three of Cups, Color: Pink
good luck	If you would rather roll the dice where your future is concerned and be surprised - so long as the surprises are pleasant, this is the opportunity for you. Tarot Card: The Star, Color: Green

Waxing	Notes
health and healing	There was a time when the healing arts were the purview and pursuit of the more spiritual-minded. In the contemporary world, commerce has brought us the perversion of alienation of our natural birthright in the sense that nothing shall be considered a remedy unless it comes in prepackaged form. Cures are corrupt because political graft in the form of pharmaceutical lobbies have made cynics of all of us. In the spirit of practical magick, wise ones continue to pass some of the precious knowledge of earth's natural healing agents to future generations however radical that may be. Use these power opportunities for spells to preserve your good health or for spells to facilitate healing. If, some malady or injury is part of your path and it can't be avoided, you can cast to ease the pain or inconvenience. Tarot Card: The World, when used as a tool in spellcraft, signifies the principle of second chances through ever-changing circumstances. The cells in the physical body are constantly reinventing themselves for better or worse. The world is a symbol of wholeness, the fruition of a goal, a project, an idea or a manifestation of desire.
high magick	As used in *Seasons* refers to spells of a more formal and elaborate nature. If you plan and execute with sincerity, this is an opportunity for one of those magickal experiences that you won't forget. Goddess: Aradia
higher learning magickal arts	Education specifically in a magickally related area whether formal or not. God: Thoth For an example of how this energy might be used, if you have been wanting a teacher and have been unable to find one who is suitable, you might cast to have a prospective mentor cross your path.

Waxing	Notes
household harmony	The three main ingredients of household harmony are balance, patience and cooperation. Naturally, for success, you must begin from an agreement within the household that harmony is a desired goal. If not, get out.

For balance of opposites, Tarot Card: The Two of Cups The suit of Cups, like the element of water, is the realm of emotion. It represents partnerhips and the balance of opposites.

For patience and/or cooperation, Tarot Card: Temperance. Temperance is almost always portrayed as a winged, female figure with an expression of marked calm. The transference of water can symbolize a healthy exchange of emotion in partner negotiations. This card can be used effectively to gain patience or to gently encourage a significant other toward a spirit of compromise. Color: Brown

Hanson-Roberts Tarot

XIV La Tempérance XIV La Temperanza
XIV Temperance
XIV Die Mässigkeit   XIV Templanza

independence	If you are working a spell for Independence, it means there are structures in place in your life that are not working in your best interest. There are several different approches that could be applied depending on your situation. If there is a form in your life that is no longer needed, an must be removed to make room for a better situation, a Tarot Card for spell focus might be The Tower as it is a symbol of deconstruction.

Waxing	Notes
independence (cont'd.)	If the issue is one of "Moving On", use Tarot Card: The Eight of Cups. This is one of the few cards that looks exactly like what it represents. Most people hold on to bad situations until the "powers that be" finally lose patience and slam the door for them. The fact that the cups are still standing implies that the figure made a proactive decision to walk away into the unknown. Color: Orange for resolve.

Hanson-Roberts Tarot

If you need to free yourself from an oppressive relationship, use Tarot Card: The Queen of Swords. She is the picture of strength, at home with her own company, she's at her best in conditions of adversity. Colors: Red for change, Orange for energy, resolve and fortitude. If your casting for independence, it's probable that you need all three.

The Queen of Swords will serve if your goal is financial independence because of her ambitious nature. Color: Green

Goddess: Diana

intuition	Spells to hone your intuition are often passed over because it sounds like work and may not seem as exciting as other aspects of the magickal arts. Developing your ability to "hear" your inner voice is as important to witchcraft as is literacy in the mundane world. Among other things, it tells you when to cast and

Waxing	Notes
intuition (cont'd.)	what to cast for. The process for developing your intuition is threefold. 1. Actively listen until you being to hear the voice. 2. Learn, usually through trial and error, how to interpret the voice. 3. Learn to trust the voice. This information comes from your source. Learning to be consistently correct in your interpretation can take a long time as interpretation is like learning another language without a guide. My first encouter with intuitive flash happened about twenty years ago. My children, a couple of their friends, and I were using a friend's beach house at Galveston. I had a brand new convertible that I had wanted for a long time and was still enjoying that rush of "new car" excitement. I got up one morning, went to the kitchen and opened the refrigerator door to start breakfast. Just then I KNEW that one of my kids (an underage driver) and his/her friend had gone out late, put my new car in neutral, pushed it down the road far enough so I wouldn't hear it start and taken it to the Sea Wall for a cruising good, glamourous joy ride. I can't say that I saw it exactly. I just knew. Two kids were wakened that day with a pretty angry mom storming the bedroom. I'm sure they will always wonder how I found out. That was when I started to listen in earnest. My sense is that the "voice" that speaks to your conscious mind through intuition is the same source that informs your subconscious mind in dreams. This energy can also be used for spells to enhance dream interpretation.

Waxing	Notes
intuition (cont'd.)	Tarot Card: The Moon s one of the most magickal and mysterious cards in the tarot. It invokes the strange and illusory world of dreams and shadow selves. Witches must venture into this landscape if we are to have the prize of highly sensitized intuition. This is one of the most elusive and advanced quests of witchcraft. Color: Lilac or Black

The Moon is the card of choice for spells to enhance intuition or to assist in meditations for the purpose of dream interpretation. When you want to interpret a troublesome dream you must return to the source for assistance in understanding the language of dreams. Dream interpretation meditations are most productive in the days of the dark moon. Candle Lilac

Card illustration from the Golden Tarot.

| investments | Yes. Witches need money, too. Spells to grow or safeguard new investments. (See also Elemental Magick. All earth spirits understand treasure. If you want to work with gnomes or dragons, you must court them over a period of time and earn their trust. They can be marvelous allies in material pursuits, but can also zap you if you ask for their help without a commitment to financial responsibility. Earth elementals also don't understand ambiguous feelings about money.)

Tarot Card: The Ace of Pentacles is a near perfect image |

Waxing	Notes
investments (cont'd.)	for an investments spell as its focus is a material gift from the All. Color: Green, of course.
job hunting	This energy is to be used for spells to light the way for a job hunt, not to be read as an astrological forecast of a good day to go on a job hunt. Tarot card: Page of Pentacles if you know the exact job you want, Wheel of Fortune if you are looking for a better situation in more general terms. Color: Green
justice	Not to be confused with revenge. This is energy for spells to insure that the good, true and right thing is accomplished in the end regardless of outcome. In other words, be certain that you are on the right side of a question before you cast a spell for justice because judgment will go in favor of the deserving party. Tarot Card: Judgment, An angel holds the Scales of Justice. On one side, a man is being pulled down by devils. On the other, small angels struggle to help a woman to restore the balance. The angel's staff is topped by a gilt owl to signify knowledge. Double-edged sword Color: White, Goddess: Cerridwen Card illustration from the Golden Tarot.

XI

JUSTICE

Waxing	Notes
magick	A magick power day is a delicious gift of all-purpose energy. All you must do is decide how best to use it. There are so many choices laid out before you right now that it may feel bewildering. But look carefully: are some of these really just daydreams or fantasies? Before you point to a menu item, discern which of these tantalising possibilities are practical propositions, and which are just tempting illusions. Tarot Card: The Seven of Cups has been called the card of "potential" which is also, perhaps, the essence of magick; requesting cooperation from the "powers that be" to manipulate physics or future events according to your desire. This is the card of dreams and imagination. In divination this card could mean a need for grounding. For spellwork, it means "What will you have?" Color: Deep Purple  Sept des Coupes Sette di Coppe **Seven of Cups** Sieben-Kelche Siete de Copas Hanson-Roberts Tarot
magnetism skills	Tarot Card: The Magician Color: Deep Purple
manifesting	Manifestation is one of magick's ways of surprising us. It can be so delightful to discover that we received what we wanted or needed in ways that we could not have imagined at the time we cast. The old metaphysical staple of constructing a "treasure map" with pictures and ideas remains one of the best magickal spells I know.

Waxing	Notes
manifesting (cont'd.)	The basic process is to first do the work of asking yourself the question, if I could have anything, what would it be? When you feel confident that you have a list, find symbols and pictorial representations. Actually do a cut and paste on poster board or in a blank book with as much "scrapbooking" technique as you want. It can't be too elaborate. Put yourself into it. Just be sure that the items you choose really engage you emotionally. In other words, don't put a new Mercedes into your treasure map just because you know the idea would be exciting to a lot of people. If it doesn't *really* engage you emotionally, not only will you not get it, but it will garble the transmission and hinder the process of getting the things you really *do* want.
	Once finished, hide it away and keep it secret. Do not show it to anyone. Think of it as a cauldron stew being covered and left to simmer. Update once a year or so.
money	For persuading Earth Elementals to work with you see Investments. For spells regarding money matters in general, Tarot Card: Ace of Pentacles Color: Green or Gold, Goddess: Freya (Vikings knew how to bring home the bacon.) or Juno Remember that spellwork takes time. If your financial need is much greater than your present net worth, results could take time. (See Sphere of Influence, Chapter 1.) This is certainly not to say you shouldn't cast for money, but that money spells should be thought of in terms beyond this month or even this year. The thing to remember is this. At the end of three years would you rather enjoy the money you cast for today or would you rather do without it? It is often easier more efficient to cast for the thing you want from the money (whether that is a material object, an essence such as recognition or a feeling of security) than to cast for money itself. See Manifesting.

Waxing	Notes
office spells	Also, workplace spells. There are lots of challenges in office situations. It has been suggested by psychologists in a recent book that one must be sociopathic to rise to the top of modern-day corporatations. To be sure, a contemplative person will find much that is disturbing. With a little magickal assistance you can do well and have your good moral character and good conscience survive at the same time. Sometimes "office spell" listings in *Seasons* are general and sometimes they are noted as particular to a situation. You have all the tools you need to devise appropriate spells and protective talismans. Also see Personal Advocacy. For promotions / raise in pay, Tarot Card: The Page of Pentacles, Color: Green For a more comfortable environment, Tarot Card: Nine of Pentacles, Color: Yellow For recognition, Tarot Card: The Knight of Wands, Color: Red For peace and stability, Tarot Card: The World, Color: Dark Blue For protection against gossip and personal sabotage, Tarot Card: The High Priestess, Color: Black
opportunity	Usually paired with "adventure" because there is so much opportunity in adventure and so much adventure in opportunity. Tarot Card: Wheel of Fortune for an unknown, The Knight of Wands when you know of a particular door you'd like opened, Color: Royal Blue
partnership, assistance	See Friendship. This is the same essence family. The same spell set applies.

Waxing	Notes
passion, sexuality	Be careful what you cast for. While sex energy is necessary to any pursuit requiring drive, force of will or charisma, it is "shadow side" work - unpredictable and highly volatile. You may experience the benefits of passion fuel, but also find yourself reaching for the "Anger Powder" much more often. If you are casting to draw fire energy (to you), or make your own flame burn hotter (into you), have the good sense and magickal maturity to build auto-controls into your spell.  XV IL DIAVOLO God: Pan (Roman Faunus) Tarot Card: The Devil. For the purpose of spellwork, The Devil represents inhibitions that do not serve you. The root of these can often be found as fear of the shadow. Many witch's believe that a fear is an unrequieted wish or desire. Fire, passion, sexuality are essential to a successful life on many levels. Color: Blood Red Illustration from the Angel Tarot.
personal advocacy	Personal advocacy spells are the magickal equivalent of "assertiveness training". The essence is "standing up for yourself". If you're not willing to fight for what you want, it's probably not really important to you. Know yourself well enough to know whether you need this or not. This energy can be used for competitions actually structured as such or for the sort of competition that involves the award of a contract or vying for a particular position in a corporate setting. Family: Fire Energy. Tarot: Seven of Wands. Color: Red

Waxing	Notes
personal finances	The distinction is made in case you have financial business interests or finances that are partly shared with someone else. This is good energy for spells to acquire sound money management skills. Problems such as overspending and neglect can be addressed. You can also use this energy for spells to improve personal wealth. If the latter is what you seek, for best results cast for that (improvement in the area of personal assets) rather than money in general or a specific amount of money. Tarot Card: The Page of Pentacles
personal magnetism	Charisma. See Attraction. Tarot Card: The Star Color depends on what you whether you want to attract love, sales, attention in general, friendship, political viability, etc. Goddess: Venus
politics, negotiation	For office politics, see Office Spells. Use this energy to enhance your communication skills and/or to make you glib. You can use the energy to cast a glamour spell so that people hear what they want to hear. Tarot Card: Seven of Swords, Color: Dark Blue.
popularity	Tarot Card: Three of Cups. You are surrounded by those who have only the best of intentions and wishes for you. Your magick design can either place you as part of the trio or you can call on t he trio to boost your attraction level. Color: Pink Life is good. Card from The Golden Tarot. ⒼHREE OF ⒸUPS

Waxing	Notes
psychic development	In the big picture, psychic development should perhaps be at the top of a witch's priority list; heightened awareness brings more abundant results to every aspect of the craft. Tarot Card: The Magician symbolizes mastery of the elements, the esoteric and the ability to channel energy or knowledge from outside the dimension of the mundane. Color Lilac, Goddess: Aradia
recognition	People need it in different forms and in varying degrees. Sometimes it seems the people who get the most recognition can never get enough, as can be evidenced by the perpetual "award shows". These people don't need spells for increased recognition. Here are a few examples of situations I imagine when citing this power energy. o if someone else is getting credit for your work o if you are not getting credit for all the work you're doing o if you are being taken for granted o if you are being overshadowed o if you are passed over for deserved praise and honors Tarot Card: Knight of Wands, Color: Orange
reflection	Time to withdraw for self-assessment and planning, taking stock of the experience you've accumulated and the lessons you've learned. What have you done well? What could be done better? Tarot Card: The Hermit, Color: Lilac
romance	Spells to call romance into your life or spells to add spice or beauty to a present relationship. This energy appears throughout the year as major and minor. Tarot Card: The Lovers, Color: Red, Goddess: Venus

Waxing	Notes
security	Protection spells go both ways. This, the waxing side of this energy, is used to erect safeguards. The shadow side is used to warn intruders away or to cast glamours to hide you from wrongdoers. Security spells are appropriate for people, animals and things. Also see, Barrier Spells for Security for spells concerning real estate and physical property. Tarot Card: The Ten of Pentacles.
self-improvement	Spells for the whole package, when you want *everything*. Tarot Card: The Empress (right) This illustration was designed for use in magick. The Empress is depicted as content, but resolute; relaxed and receptive, but committed to her personal truth. The light in her eyes is fueled by the power of magickal knowledge. Fertility is expressed by the lush greenery in the background. The ability to manifest at will (ease in birthing her desires) is expressed by the waterfall that rushes by. Her crown is made of gold and platinum to indicate the security of manmade assets, but fashioned in the form of a laurel wreath to mean a primal connection to nature. The luxuriant mass of thick, shiny hair serves as a beacon of attraction because it is read by the subconscious mind to mean health, youth and vitality. The Bergere chair and the deep folds in the clothing are read as wealth. The heart at her feet is red and vibrant, but not perfect or naive. The female symbol within the heart has been recreated as a rose in full bloom. The scepter that leans against her chair indicates the power always readily available, within easy grasp. That power, always readily available, is yours to claim in witchcraft for so long as it is used wisely and used well.

The Empress

Waxing	Notes
shapeshift-ing	An excellent example of a magickal irony. Shapeshifting is extremely complex and advanced magick. Definitely not for beginners because of highly unstable energies and unpredictable outcomes and yet beginners are often attracted because of the drama and glamour. There are two distinct forms. One is symbolic of major shifts in an individual's circumstance or personality. The other is more literal, the actual metamorphosis of human to other being as described in *The Once and Future King*. In native American cultures the phenomenon is drug induced while experienced and sympathetic elders monitor. Shapeshifting can be literal, particularly when working in the Astral, but is most often meant to be read as transformative work. In that sense, the Death card can be helpful in expediting changes. Death is most often thought to have negative connotations and, while sometimes it may, it more often represents an end immediately followed by a new beginning - just as it does in dreams. It very rarely means actual physical death. For permanent shifts, use Tarot Card: Death. This card is a powerful, magickal tool for creating dramatic shifts; ex. divorce, moves, career changes, weight loss, breaking addictions or bad habits. Color: Black For glamours (advanced craft) use Tarot Card: The Moon with caution regarding its unpredictable nature. It can reflect and turn the glamour on you. Color: Deep Purple, Goddess: Arianhrod
social success	Similar to popularity, but further reaching. When creating a spell for social success here are things to keep in mind. The accomplished witch knows well that a successful spell begins with correctly identifying the essence of the desire. It is this desire, ground and pressed

Waxing	Notes
social success (cont'd.)	down that generates energy sufficient to rearrange physical reality. What is the goal of social success? That essence might be as simple as company or as complicated as recognition or business opportunities arising from social success. Colors: Companionship: Pink Emotional Connection:Lilac Recognition: Orange Business Networking: Green Sales: Gold
solitary magick	There is indeed a time for everything including the quiet power of solitary magicks. Some of us find that our most potent and memorable results were generated by spells cast in the solemnity of solitude. Above all, take steps to be certain you are not disturbed during your ritual. **THE MAGICIAN.** Tarot Card: The Magician, Color: Deep Purple Goddess: Aradia Rider Waite Deck
stretch time	You are aware that sometimes time flies and sometimes it drags. You don't always have to be a victim of chance in this regard. Although you can't actually stretch time, you can increase your productivity so that the result is the same. Difficult for the beginner, but worth the effort to learn. This is one of those magickal skills which will go "auto" once perfected, meaning that eventually you can create a shift with little more than a passing thought. Tarot Card: Two of Rods, Color: Yellow

Waxing	Notes
success	Often paired with "ambition" because success has come to be generally understood in terms of professional or material achievement. If you are ambitious, but find that success eludes you, The Emperor is your card. The Emperor's expression is usually stern like that of a disciplinarian. To be sure, success usually requires a good measure of self-discipline, as does the practice of magick. Color: Gold / Yellow
travel	Applies to the sort of trip that broadens your experience and raises your consciousness. Often called a vacation, it should be called education. Unless you specifically want to cruise or sail, invoke the powers of "air". Travel Spells (Pleasure) Tarot Card: The Eight of Wands speaks to the subconcious on the essence of flight and the personal growth that accompanies new experience. Send the essence of this card ahead into the smoky realm of "substance not yet formed" to manifest a dream trip. Travel Spells (Business) Tarot Card: The Knight of Wands Color appropriate to the essence of that which you wish to gain from travel.
vigor	See Health and Healing. Use when you need more zest or energy.
warrior energy	Fortune does favor the brave. Warrior energy and courage most often appear as a pair, but they are not the same thing. Warrior energy is the fuel that feeds the courage. Tarot Card: Seven of Wands Candle Color: Red, Goddess: Freya
work in the astral	Some theorists hold that rumors of witches flying arose from the ability to teleport one's essence by astral means. Watch for cautions regarding the use of electricity. Goddess: Hecate

Waxing	Notes
work in B.O.S.	If you want to use a card for focus when working in your Book of Shadows, that would be the High Priestess. She rules the subconcious realm of esoteric knowledge and the worldly realm of wisdom. She is often depicted holding a book or scroll to symbolize guardianship of hidden truths. This card is brimming with magickal symbols to inspire work in your Book of Shadows. Color: Lilac See Chapter 9.

The High Priestess, Jessica Galbreth

Waning Energy

As in applied art, the shadow is as important as the light.

Every energy has a counterpart. Sometimes energies are opposite and sometimes they are two approaches to the same result using different moon phases to get there.

Opposites

WAXING	WANING
elemental magick	banish unwanted entities
magick (general)	reversals
manifesting	repelling
romance	amicable divorce or parting

There is an ancient adage that, if something is worth doing, it's worth doing right. It applies here in the sense that, if you have an issue of importance, you can double your influence by addressing it from both its sides.

Two Sides of the Same Thing

WAXING	WANING
domestic harmony	resolve domestic issues
health and healing	banish sickness, disease
money	eliminate obstacles to wealth
success	break down barriers

Waning	Notes
amicable divorce or parting	Time to move on. You now need to make a physical or psychological move away from a situation that's been going on for far too long. While this can be positive, it may initially be tiring and dispiriting to actually take this step. However, the weariness you feel is actually a sign that you need to change things and get away from what has now become a routine or a fruitless habit. Don't be afraid to take that first step. It will get easier, and one day you will look back and be glad you had the courage to make this change. An exception to the usual cautions regarding the magickal manipulation of another individual's emotions. If a relationship cannot be saved and no purpose can be served by enmity, cast a spell to ease the transition for both of you as far in advance of the break-up as possible.

Huit des Coupes   Otto di Coppe
Eight of Cups
Acht-Kelche   Ocho de Copas

banishings	*Banish negative energy, influences, enemies, forces.* First, try to identify the nature of the disturbance. Salt, smoke and besoms work with efficiency and immediacy in the Netherworld. For home clearing method, see Chapter 8 - Clearing the Space. *Obstacles to career goals, success.* This sort of banishing is relatively easy. All you *must* have is a black candle and a waning moon. If the obstacle is a person, you can have your cake and eat it, too by banishing them to the realization of their dream, whatever that might be, as long as it's someplace else.

Waning	*Notes*
banishings (cont'd).	*Sickness, disease, addiction.* Cast for yourself or for others, but only with the express permission of the afflicted. There could be fatalistic reasons for their experience. Tarot Card: Nine of Swords crossed by Strength, Color: Orange, Goddess: Hecate *Debt* - Counter with spells to compel yourself toward money management - then cast for relief.
bindings	One of my favoties. I only have to use it once in a decade, or so, but it's so nice to have in my magick tool kit. Spells of Binding are controversial among witches who are also Wiccan as they are thought to be a possible infraction of the "harm none" directive of The Rede. However, some of us hold the opinion that a binding will have no effect on someone who is being wrongly judged by you. In other words, if you're right, they have it coming. If you're wrong, no harm done. Whether you are for or against, a binding spell should not be undertaken lightly and certainly not by the young or by absolute beginners as wisdom and maturity are required to determine whether it is necessary or not. Bindings, in my experience, work faster than any other spell. If done properly you will see results within a day. Tarot Card: The Eight of Swords is an excellent card to assist you in a spell of binding because the imagery is appropriate to your goal and appeals to both conscious and subconscious. The figure is blindfolded and bound, though not so tightly that she couldn't break free (as should be the case in a righteous binding). For your purposes, the blindfold may symbolize loss of certainty of one's position or viewpoint. Make a note on a future date to release the subject to go their way in peace. Or, better yet, build a release into your spell to the effect that, when the object of the spell is willing to entertain the notion that all points of view are valid at least or that (s)he is wrong at best, then (s)he will be free.

Waning	Notes
break down barriers	An all-purpose, destruction spells to be used for blocks artificially erected by culture or experience. Tarot Card: The Devil. This card in a spread or reading most often indicates a dilemma of the querant's choosing. It's probably judicious to avoid using The Devil in spellwork because the mixed messages, symbols, imagery, etc. could take you on a magickal tangent or in the wrong direction entirely, but there are exceptions to every rule. Do not use in magick UNLESS you are using the card to free yourself of unwanted barriers and you have mastered sufficient concentration to hold an image of breaking free for at least one full minute.
chaos protection	Some kinds of chaos are marvelous. One example being the disturbance of earth and rearrangement caused by new planting. While absolutely necessary to the big picture, chaos is more pleasant under the controlled conditions of deliberate transition. Without your consent chaos can exact a price upon your well-being in terms of health and, sometimes, relationships. Perhaps we should say "protection from unwanted chaos". Invoke the goddess Ma'at for the wisdom to know when to initiate a change and for balance and order as you do.

Chaos

Waning	Notes
defend against psychic attack	Someone may wish you harm either consciously or subconsciously. That doesn't mean they have the power to curse you. Chances are slim that they do. But, it can be hard to tell and as Ben Franklin said writing as Poor Richard, "An ounce of prevention is worth a pound of cure."As a young woman I had occasion to work with the daughter of the Egyptian ambassador to Austria. She had spent her entire life in Vienna, but when you scratched the surface you found an Egyptian. I asked her once about a brooch she always wore and she told me a story which I think of as the Amulet of the Evil Eye.
	I should interrupt my story to mention that my friend had striking, almond shaped eyes that much like those often depicted in Egyptian ancient art. She had been at a party when she was in her late teens. A woman had made a point of complimenting her beautiful eyes, but the compliment did not *feel* sincere. The next day, when she woke, her eyes were swollen almost shut from what appeared to be a severe allergical reaction. She said she had the look of a boxer who had taken a lot of punches to the eye area. The condition persisted for several days during which she declined to be seen in public.
	In her mind, there is no question that she was a victim of "evil eye", a curse which can be invoked deliberately or by unconscious, but severe, jealousy. After that experience she acquired an amulet charmed for the purpose of protecting her from "evil eye". She told me to be wary of people who give compliments because one can never know the true heart of another. Maybe their words are a gift. Maybe their words are a curse. Since it is her people who invented the magicks of the mystery schools and perhaps others as well, I did not take the tale lightly.
	Tarot Card: The High Priestess, BEWARE: This card

Waning	Notes
defend against psychic attack (cont'd.)	will bite! Use with caution. If your intention is to effect the will of others, this is a card that will turn on you in a hurry. Use to deflect (or boomerang) negative energy. Color: Black
discourage a would-be lover	This applies to harmless pests as well as stalkers. You may never need power energy such as this, but, if you should, it's nice to know it's available. Use to repel the more dangerous predators, but also to dismiss others without being forced to be unkind. Tarot: The Queens are very powerful tools in all areas of love. The Queen of Wands can be used for spells to attract and seduce or, tuned upside down, for the opposite effect - to send away. If someone is pressing you with unwanted attention, send the darker side of the Queen of Wands. Goddess: Athena
eliminate obstacles to wealth, power or fame	Magick works for worldly pursuits as well as for more idealized endeavors. The idea is "do what you came here for". Tarot Card: The Five of Wands represents struggle and challenge. For spells to eliminate obstacles of any kind use The Five of Wands and cross it with a talisman, a symbol of protection or The Nine of Cups. Color: green for wealth, red for power, orange for fame

Queen of Wands

Waning	Notes
initiate endings	Spells to initiate endings. (See vacuum effect, p. 82.) You must make room for the new essence you want to create by letting go of that which no longer serves you. Setting the wheels in motion magickally will help the transition go smoother and help set your commitment. Tarot Card: Death represents the end of a cycle, rebirth, transformation. All witches are familiar with the principle of death and renewal in nature. The same applies to every part of our lives. Color: Deep Purple
protection (general)	Spells to protect must be renewed fairly often because they are particularly susceptible to magickal entropy. (With the exception of Barrier Spells for Security, p90.) Cast after dark when possible. Wear black. Use black candles to protect things. Light purple or silver candles to protect essences. White candles to protect people. Let them burn until first light of the morrow even if you have to transfer tham to the bathtub for safety's sake. To use the tarot as a tool in protection spells, either choose your significator (the card that represents you in traditional systems of tarot divination) or a card that represents the thing or essence you wish to protect. Lay this card in an east-west direction with the head in the east and cross it (horizontally, head in north) with a card that represents good outcome, talisman or sacred symbol. If you are in a hurry, in a crowd or some other situation that requires a kiss and a blessing, just close your eyes and picture light beginning at the core of the object of protection and emanating outward and upward. Assign the light protective (barrier) qualities and set it in motion stirring clockwise, slowly around the object, three times. Stop the motion, but leave the light in place. Renew when you think about it. Assume the thought is a prompt to renew.

Waning	Notes
release unwanted emotion	Spells that release unproductive emotions can put you in touch with a well of reserves and free up energy for better use. These emotions cannot be fully extinguished, but can be redirected into productive channels. If not addressed then, like stress, negative emotion eats away at good bodily health and good perspective as well. Tarot Card: Strength is a symbol of inner resources, learning to live in harmony with our shadow selves. The lion symbolizes the beastly and destructive side of our nature which must be embraced if we are to reap the rewards of self-acceptance. Color: Brown or White Card from Hanson-Roberts Tarot.

VIII La Force   VIII La Forza
VIII Strength
VIII Die Kraft   VIII Fuerza

relieve stress	Tarot Card: Six of Swords, Color: Brown
repelling magicks	Use magickal means to repel anything unwanted. This energy is even effective for a "get rid of" list. Repelling magick is not the same thing as spells of destruction which, by the way, you rarely need. Most annoyances can simply be sent away. *Note: There is also a distinction between Repelling Magick and Reversals. Reversals, as the term indicates, require that something done be undone. This energy can be used for either type of magick even though the approach is different.*

Waning	Notes
resolve domestic issues	An example of a repelling spell. This spell is designed to move an issue aside and not to get your way. To get your way, use energy for domestic power. Resolve domestic issues spells are most effective when paired with a cross-current waxing energy such as household harmony. Tarot: CROSS the Nine of Swords with the Ace of Cups. This is effectively replacing negative thoughts with a gift of peace. Candle Color. Brown
reversals	When this energy emerges, it is an opportunity to reverse magick that went awry or produced effects not intended. You can also effectively use this energy for "uncrossings", reversing hexes or other forms of psychic attack. Basically, the more serious the situation, the more painstaking you should be in your preparation. Carve pentacles into as many black candles (unscented) as you want to use. A long time ago, when I was much younger, but still old enough to know better, I thought perhaps I could sneak in the back door of the Rule of Three. This was not a working for myself, but for someone dear to me. I thought I had all the right reasons behind me. So I designed a spell to make someone go away by causing their means of employment to be cut off. My back door was to also create a marvelous and attractive opportunity to open up for them somewhere else. I used a combination spell that involved kitchen witchery. It proved to be extremely powerful, only it didn't have any effect them. Within twelve hours, my own source of income was being threatened. I reversed that working in a hurry. As it turned out, it would not have been for the best for that person to be sent away. I guess I'm not all-knowing after all. The long and short of it is that everything

Waning	Notes
	you've been told about spells intended to effect specific other people is true. Such a spell is self-sabotage. The good news is that the powers-that-be forgiving of magicks gone awry. If you put as much or more energy into the reversal as the original working, you shouldn't have too much trouble undoing the damage. Even if you are not reckless enough to defy every tenet of practical magick, there may be occasions when your magick was innocent enough, but just went the wrong direction. If that happens, keep a good accounting of it and do a reversal.

Chapter 12 References

The Ancient Elements

Earth	North or East
Air	East or South
Fire	South or West
Water	West or North

Moon Phases

WAXING	BEGINS
New Moon	time noted in Seasons
Crescent	3 1/2 days after New Moon
1st Quarter	3 1/2 days after Crescent
Gibbous	3 1/2 days after 1st Quarter
Full Moon	3 1/2 days after Gibbous

WANING	BEGINS
Disseminating	3 1/2 days after Full Moon
Last Quarter	3 1/2 days after Disseminating
Balsamic (Dark Moon)	3 1/2 days after Last Quarter

Book of Shadows Esbat Blessing

I summon the Lady and the Lord
Bless this book as I record..

Ancient spinnings, spirits bind
from prying eyes and other kind.

Those who would read my book of days
see blotches, smears, indecipherable haze.

Guardian East, Almighty Wind
Bring forth thy powers, my book defend
from magick core to seeing eyes
knowledge herein make me wise.

Guardian South, Keeper of Flames
I summon you in all your names.
Find this book upon my death
as I shall give up my last breath.

Guardian West, Ruler of the Sea,
Bless this Book times three times three.
Sail my ship on holy water
this your gift to Avalon's daughter.

Guardian North, Great Dragon Grael,
I conjure you from head to tail.
Made from trees grown in your earth
I invite you to the birth

of this my book of shadow and light
dedicated on this full moon night.

Seasons Witches' Year Lunar Calendar

The first day of the Witches' Lunar Year occurs on the new moon before Samhain. That would be Phasma Priscus 1. All thirteen months only appear during years with thirteen moons. That would be once every two to three years. In other years Alban Heruin will not appear.

Phasma Priscus	Days of ancient spirits
Shamash	Days of the witch gods
Grael	Days of the Earth dragon
Imbolgen	Days of Reclamation
Keowulf	Days of the Old Ones
Raven	Days of Air
Annwyn	Days of Avalon
Mab	Days of Faerie
Alban Heruin	Days of the Druid (years with 13 moon cycles)
Faunus	Days of Pan
Lugnasadh	Days of Lug
Belz	Days of Fire
Blodlessing	Days of Harvest Rites

Wheel of the Year
Gregorian 200_ / Witches Calendar

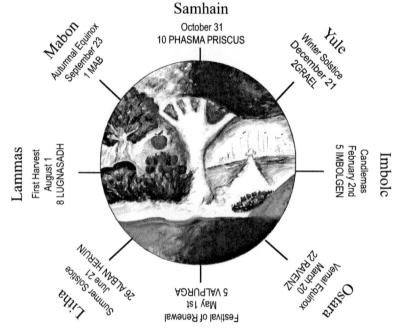

Samhain
October 31
10 PHASMA PRISCUS

Mabon
Autumnal Equinox
September 23
1 MAB

Yule
Winter Solstice
December 21
2 GRAEL

Lammas
First Harvest
August 1
8 LUGNASADH

Imbolc
Candlemas
February 2nd
5 IMBOLGEN

Litha
Summer Solstice
June 21
26 ALBAN HERUIN

Beltane
Festival of Renewal
May 1st
5 VALPURGA

Ostara
Vernal Equinox
March 20
22 RAVENZ

ESBATS	200_	Witches' Months	
Still Moon	January 3	KEOWULF	
Talisman Moon	February 2	IMBOLGEN	
Gathering of the Clan Moon	March 3	RAVEN	Wishing Moon
Moon of the Celtic Cross	April 2	ANNWYN	
Shapeshifter Moon	May 2	MAB	
Blue Moon	May 31	ALBAN HERUIN	
Fire Moon	June 11	FAUNUS	Wishing Moon
Warrior Moon	July 10	LUGNASADH	
Dark Moon	August 9	BELZ	
Offerring Moon	September 7	BLODLESSING	Wishing Moon
Shadows Moon	October 6	PHASMA PRISCUS	
Moon of the Silver Cord	November 5	SHAMASH	
Mystic Moon	December 4	GRAEL	Wishing Moon

Witches's Holy Days

As a rule witches honor nature. Even Cyberwitches notice the change of seasons. Based on the reconstruction of the Old Ways of Western European pagans, there are eight festivals, or Sabbats, that mark the year as it moves through a revolution of seasons. This cycle is often called the Wheel of the Year"; the eight festivals each representing a spoke.

The four major sabbats are important astronomical events. The four minor sabbats help mark time and occasions.

The four major sabbats, high holy days, are:
- the day of shortest light, Yule
- the day of longest light, Litha
- two days of equal day and night: Ostara and Mabon

The four minor sabbats occur on fixed dates at cross-quarter points, each halfway between the major Sabbats

Expressed in linear form, the year looks like this.

Samhain	cross-quarter	fixed date	October 31
Yule	**Winter Solstice**	**around**	**December 21**
Imbolc	cross-quarter	fixed date	February 2
Ostara	**Spring Equinox**	**around**	**March 22**
Beltane	cross-quarter	fixed date	May 1
Litha	**Summer Solstice**	**around**	**June 21**
Lammas	cross-quarter	fixed date	August 1
Mabon	**Fall Equinox**	**around**	**September 22**

The first page of *Seasons of the Witch* is always a representation of the Wheel of the Year with exact Sabbat dates for that year followed by the year's Esbats or full moons.

Detailed notes on lore and tradition can be found on or next to every Sabbat thoughtout your planner.

The Shadow Magicks of Reflective Surfaces

There is little in the world more magickal than surfaces that reflect. They are conductors and magnifiers of light, dark and ambiguities. Sometimes they merely increase images. Sometimes they reverse images. Sometimes they distort images. The question of using reflective surfaces is one that should be considered in the planning and implementation of spells. Be aware of reflective surfaces, their properties and what, exactly, they will reflect. By this I mean that your TV screen, when turned off, becomes a reflective surface as do glass coverings on artwork and a myriad of other things.

To identify what will reflect during a working, you must, when possible, duplicate conditions as anticipated during the time of your casting. Test the light that you plan to use. Some things reflect in some light and not others. This isn't always possible because sometimes there are surprises. For instance, I live in a semitropical area where heavy thunderstorms can come and go in a hurry on a day that is otherwise bright and sunny. These storms bring black clouds that cover my sky with such darkness as to simulate night time. Under these conditions I can begin a spell in bright light and end with none.

Reflective surfaces can multiply your effect, alter your purpose or even reverse your intention. The only way you can be sure which is which is to -

1. **be aware of the nature and location of reflective surfaces particularly in the case of materials that distort reflected images**. If you discover a reflection that is distorting something pertinent to your spell, you could cast a charm over the object but it would be so much easier to simply cover the surface with a cloth, turn it around, move it, or whatever resolves the issue.

2. **take it into account**

3. **incorporate it into your plans, make it a tool assigned with deliberate intention to do this or that**

Light and Shadow Aspects of Color

If you are working with candle magick, pay particularly close attention because there is a magickal excitation at work when flame is reflected (thereby doubled). On the question of candle color, I have devised this chart to help you discern the integrated personalities of color. Every color has a shadow side to its personality.

COLOR	*LIGHT*	*SHADOW*
black	protection, banishing, disguise, magick	evil, destruction, paranoia, deceit
white	idealism, ethics, virtue	vulnerability, weakness, self-righteousness
pale purple	truth, spirituality, intuition, clairvoyance	hypocrisy, sanctimony, self-righteousness
deep purple	creativity, astral projection, shapeshifting, magick	fear, illogic, power over others
yellow	home, hearth, health	structural breakdown of body and/or environment, cruelty, sadism
orange	resolve, fortitude, stamina, balanced ego	danger, misjudgment, distraction, self-doubt, mental illness
red	passion, strength, courage, sexuality, change	foolhardiness, tactlessness, gambling, sociopathy
brown	domestic tranquility, peace, romanticism, balance	self-sabotage, selfishness, insatiability
green	money, luck, fertility	sickness, insecurity, hypersensitivity
sea blue	compassion, flexibility, meditation	insubstantiability, disharmony
dark blue	stability, politics, intellect	apathy, conformity, complacence

God(esse)s Who Are Particularly Sympathetic to Witches

Aradia - (Roman) Queen and Protector of Witches
Daughter of Diana and Lucifer. Aradia was sent to live in human form here on Earth. Diana spoke to her daughter saying, "A mortal thou must go to Earth below, to be a teacher unto women and men who fain would study witchcraft in thy school."[1] This, of course, predates the Christ myth, but the similarity of gods sending offspring to live in mortal form for the benefit of humanity originated here.

Arianrhod (Celtic)
Mother aspect of the Welsh Triple Goddess, her name means Silver Wheel. She is associated with the celestial realms, believed to be the waiting place of the spirits of the dead. Along with her attendants Arianrhod decides fates of the departed. She is often depicted with silver wheels, a white chariot and a sheaf of wheat. She is invoked for Moon Magick, Death, Rebirth, Wheel of the Year and Fertility.

Brigid (Celtic)
a.k.a. Bride, Bridey, Brighid, Brigit, Briggidda, Brigantia

> *I am She*
> *that is the natural*
> *mother of all things,*
> *mistress and governess*
> *of all the elements,*
> *the initial progeny of worlds,*
> *chief of the powers divine,*
> *Queen of all that are in the otherworld,*
> *the principal of them*
> *that dwell above,*
> *manifested alone*
> *and under one form*
> *of all the Gods and Goddesses.*

> - Lucius Apuleius

[1] *Gospel of the Witches*, 1899, controversial book by Charles Godfrey Leland

Brigid is particularly germane to modern witches because she is thought to be the bridge between Celtic-based branches of witchcraft and the Old Ways. Her reputation for traveling between worlds makes her particularly sympathetic to witches on quest in other dimensions and for scholarly witches who seek to restore and preserve a history of magick. She is supreme god to midwives and healers. In a version of "if you can't beat them, join them" she was made saint by Christians because the Irish, who could be persuaded to relinquish most pagan practices, would not budge regarding worship of Brigid. Invoke for domestic matters.

Cerridwen (Celtic)

The Old One of triple aspect. Patron goddess of femininity and justice whose symbol is the sacred cauldron.

Diana (Greek, Artemis)

Roman goddess of the hunt, Patroness of Dianic Witchcraft, Goddess of modern Feminism. Greek counterpart, Artemis. Hunter of the gods, Diana is guardian of nature and all things wild. She is the moon goddess, twin sister of Apollo, the sun god. When GrecoRoman mythology was conceived the two heavenly bodies were thought to be equal representations of day and night because, from earth's perspective, both appear to be about the size of a quarter.

In one of mythology's most precious stories, the child Diana gives her father, Zeus, a list of things she wanted for her third birthday. She asked to be allowed to live without the distractions of love or marriage, for a bow and arrow like Apollo's, for hunter's dress and freedom from the demands of feminine dress, for the job of bringing light into the world, for sixty young nymphs to be companions and care for her dogs, and for all the mountains on the earth to live on.

In art she is usually depicted with bow and arrow or carrying a torch or candle. An excellent ally in any spell involving independence, strength, warrior energy, competition or resolve.

Freya (Norse)

Wife of Odin. Goddess of magick and divination. Also, fertility, war and wealth.

Hecate (Greek)

Goddess of crossroads and patroness of witches' meetings there. She has come to be patroness of Samhain. Most commonly known as the Crone face of the Triple Goddess. Like her origin she is as mysterious as her name which has several meanings including "She who works her will", "One from afar", and "Most Shining One". This suggests her power is multi-faceted and far reaching. According to the Sibyl of Cumue (*Aeneid*), Hecate held control of the Avernus Wood, the entrance to Hades (Greek Underworld). Medea called herself the daughter of Hecate.

Hecate is a "passage goddess", the "Guardian of Doorways", who watched over birth and death, and the guide of the Initiates who dared to pass between the worlds. She is feared simply because transitions are feared.

She is still invoked as the patroness of all who stand on the boundary between life and death, such as midwives, healers and all witches on occasion. She is also called upon when working with the dark moon, any time of transition, the unknown and spells of protection.

Isis (Egyptian)

Skill in the practice of magick. Patron goddess of medicine and domestic matters.

Juno (Roman)

Goddess of money.

Ma'at (Egyptian)

Feminine counterpart of Thoth. Patron goddess of order and truth.

Pan (Greek, Faunus)

The satyr god, or demigod, of the forest, of shepherds, of dance and sex, and love of earthy passions; the primitive's version of Dionysus. Pan was morphed into "The Devil" of Christian fame. Images of witches deep in the forest, dancing around a fire with Pan arouse deep seated fears in some religious sects. Pan is often depicted playing a reed flute now known as Panpipes.

Qetesh (Egyptian)

Goddess of sexuality.

Theia (Titan)

Goddess of "sight" and divination.

Thoth (Eyptian)

Egyptian creator of magick. Patron of knowledge, secrets and writing. Messenger to other gods, similar to Greek Hermes, but also mediator and counselor to the gods. Like most gods of magick, he was associated with the moon and is frequently depicted wearing a crescent moon on his head. Invoke Thoth for spells to resolve disputes, for written communication and to assist in the writing or creation of spells or rituals.

Venus (Greek, Aphrodite)

Daughter of Jupiter and Dione. She is Goddess of sexual love, beauty, grace and gardens. Venus inspires compassion and appreciation for all that is beautiful around us. She lives in every woman and man. Her gift is that of sensuality and emotion. Venus rises within us whenever we see or feel something of beauty.

Chapter 13 Afterword

Index

For more information on *Seasons in Avalon* School of Magick and Traditional Craft, visit 7th-House.com or

www.**Witch-School**.com

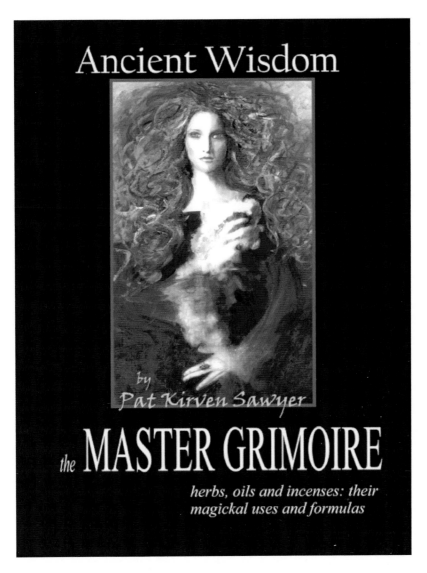

Ancient Wisdom

by
Pat Kirven Sawyer

the MASTER GRIMOIRE

herbs, oils and incenses: their
magickal uses and formulas

<u>*The*</u> *Definitive Magickal Cookbook*

Complete compendium of herbs, oils, and incenses for ritual ingredients, baths, tinctures, perfumes, sachets. Magickal applications include candle magick technique and annointing oil, powders, potions, floorwashes, talismans, charms and enchantments. $26.95

KELLY DANANN

Tarot
Magick

a Seasons of the Witch
companion guide

Using the Tarot for magickal purposes. In FULL color. $19.95

the *Witches' dictionary*

by Victoria David Danann

Sometimes you just need the short answer. $9.95

FAVORITE TOOL OF WITCHES EVERYWHERE
In FULL color. $19.95 to $34.95   from 7th-House.com